Victorian Los Angeles

Victorian LOS ANGELES

From Pio Pico to Angels Flight

CHARLES EPTING

THE History PRESS

Published by The History Press
Charleston, SC 29403
www.historypress.net

First published 2015

Manufactured in the United States

ISBN 978.1.62619.608.7

Library of Congress Control Number: 2014958799

This book is dedicated to my brothers in the Beta Tau Chapter of Theta Chi Fraternity.

"Stand fast, stand firm, stand sure, stand true."

–Harrison Gray Otis (1837–1917),

Publisher, Los Angeles Times

CONTENTS

Preface

"Victorian Los Angeles" may be something of a misnomer—or, at the very least, a title that is practically undefinable. The Victorian era is a historical concept that has both a literal and a colloquial definition. Queen Victoria herself, for whom the ubiquitous era is named, ruled from 1837 to 1901; therefore, a technical definition of the Victorian era would encompass only those years.

However, ask most people to think of a Victorian house or Victorian clothing, and certain images will come to mind, regardless of specific dates. This is the connotative definition of the Victorian era—things that we have come to associate with the reign of Victoria through popular depictions of the era. Plenty of Victorian-style homes, for example, were constructed after 1901, and many men continued to wear top hats past that date despite their association with the Victorian era.

When I began to research this book, I was unsure which approach I was going to take. The first major problem I came across was the futility of trying to apply the technical dates of the Victorian era to any aspect of American history—particularly somewhere so far removed from the Crown as Los Angeles. The dates 1837 and 1901 are completely arbitrary confines to place on California, as Victoria's ascension to the throne and death had little to no impact on the daily lives of people in Los Angeles.

At the same time, Los Angeles's period of traditionally Victorian architecture was extremely short-lived; likewise, the city's history as a Wild West town prevented Los Angeles from embracing Victorian societal norms to the extent that other large American cities did. To therefore focus exclusively on the stereotypically "Victorian" aspects of Los Angeles would not have provided a compelling historical narrative.

The approach I took for this book is somewhere between the two ends of the spectrum. The temporal range of this book is, roughly, 1837 to 1901; however, significant events that occurred before or after these dates have not been excluded because of an arbitrary technicality. Within those years, I have paid special attention to the more typical aspects of Victorian culture as it is perceived today—Queen Anne architecture, pleasure gardens and high society.

As it turned out, the confines of 1837 to 1901 worked remarkably well for Los Angeles. In the late 1830s and early 1840s, the city was experiencing the last vestiges of its Mexican Period as the stage was being set for war. Conflict finally arrived in 1846, only nine years after Victoria's reign began.

More important, though, is what coincided with the end of the Victorian era. Within about a decade on either side of 1901, three major events changed Los Angeles immeasurably. First, Edward Doheny discovered oil in 1892, and this revolutionized Los Angeles's economy and brought a new prominence to the fledgling city. Second, the year 1910 saw the birth of the movie industry in Hollywood with the filming of D.W. Griffith's *In Old California*. Lastly, in 1913, the Los Angeles Aqueduct was completed, providing Los Angeles with the necessary infrastructure to develop into a true metropolis.

The occurrence of all three of these events within a relatively short period represented a marked shift in the history of the city. Construction increased exponentially, and many buildings from the nineteenth century were deemed antiquated and demolished. The demographics of the city changed rapidly. Almost overnight, a city that had been the same for more than half a century—in essence, if not in actuality—was transformed.

Most of downtown's landmarks, from the Art Deco city hall to Grauman's Million Dollar Theater to the Central Branch of the Los Angeles Public Library, are a direct result of this shift during the first decades of the twentieth century. For most residents, these buildings are representative of Los Angeles's history, as (with very few exceptions) there is simply nothing older than them left. Although undoubtedly historic, these buildings represent only a small slice of Los Angeles's history and do not come close to telling the whole story.

A typical example of this phenomenon—the "new" Los Angeles eclipsing the old—can be seen with the downtown Los Angeles Public Library.

Threatened with demolition in 1978, the library's preservation was ensured by the formation of the Los Angeles Conservancy, which has since continued to fight for particular buildings throughout the county.

Today, the public library is heralded as one of the most impressive success stories of the preservationist movement in Los Angeles and serves as a model for other such initiatives. It is an age-old tale—new development threatens the historic and cultural fabric of a community, and the members of said community band together to protect their collective past. Grass-roots activism prevails and everyone is happy.

However, few people realize that the Central Library was, at one time, a modern development itself. Since 1882, the site had been occupied by the State Normal School, the forerunner to the University of California–Los Angeles (UCLA). With its Gothic architecture that "impressed passers-by with arched windows and decorative pinnacles," the State Normal School was a stalwart of the Los Angeles skyline for several decades.

I often wonder what public response was like when the school was demolished to make way for the modern public library, whose architecture combined exotic influences from Byzantine, Egyptian and Spanish traditions. I would be shocked if there weren't certain old-fashioned types who resented the radical and revolutionary building replacing their beloved Victorian architecture—much in the same way that the Los Angeles Conservancy would have resented a modern high-rise replacing the beloved library.

History is in the eye of the beholder, but when all one can see are products of the twentieth century, it is difficult to contextualize the history of a city as large as Los Angeles. This book is intended to fill in that gap that is so underrepresented today—the Los Angeles that we can only see through scattered remains across the county.

Covering more than sixty years of history in a city as large as Los Angeles is no easy task, and much longer books have been written on much more specific topics than this one. Therefore, this book should not be thought of as exhaustive or comprehensive by any means; instead, I have tried to give a representative sample of what the city was like during the nineteenth century. For example, there are dozens, if not hundreds, of Queen Anne/Victorian homes that easily could have been included in this book because of their architectural or historic merit.

Doing so, however, not only would have been overwhelming and redundant, but it would have been against my intended purpose for this book as well. Instead of conducting a purely academic survey of Victorian

Los Angeles, I wanted to take readers inside Victorian Los Angeles, trying as best I can to convey what life was actually like so long ago.

By presenting each chapter as a series of isolated vignettes, I have tried to cover as much ground as possible—geographically, temporally and thematically. There are undoubtedly things I have missed that perhaps should have been included, but as with any book with such a vast scope, compressing more than six decades of history into such a small space is never easy.

I have enjoyed learning as much as possible about Victorian Los Angeles, and I hope you do too. Thank you for joining me on this journey.

Acknowledgements

First and foremost, I'd like to thank everyone who supported me during the research and writing process, including my parents, my sister, my nana, my cousin David and my fellow USC students—without your constant enthusiasm and encouragement, this book never would have been possible.

I'd also like to thank all the institutions that helped provide material for my research, including (but not limited to) the Santa Monica Public Library, the University of California Library, the *Los Angeles Times* archive and the Los Angeles Public Library.

CHAPTER 1

THE EARLY VICTORIAN ERA, 1837–1848

LOS ANGELES IN THE 1830s

The early history of Los Angeles has been covered numerous times in the past, and to chronicle the Spanish and early Mexican eras of the city is beyond the scope of this book. Although the technical start of the Victorian era, 1837, is more or less arbitrary with regards to Los Angeles in particular, the 1830s did represent a transitional period for the city, and that is where this book will begin.

By the 1830s, the entire population of Los Angeles consisted of only about eight hundred people. When Los Angeles was founded in the late 1700s, it was designated as a pueblo (the Spanish term for a civilian settlement, as opposed to religious missions and military presidios); however, it would take until 1835 for Los Angeles to be declared an official city by the Mexican government. Of the eight hundred residents, a vast majority were Native American or Hispanic, with only a few dozen being of other European background.

For the most part, in the days before the Mexican-American War, Los Angeles retained much of the character it had as a Spanish pueblo. The Plaza continued to be the economic and cultural hub of the city, which was steadily growing at a rate of about twenty-five people per year. There were, however, growing tensions within Alta California at this time, with many

Los Angeles residents vying to take control of the territory away from its capital, Monterey. This is reflected in the rapid succession of governors of Alta California in the middle and latter parts of the 1830s.

It was also during this time that some of Los Angeles's modern neighborhoods began taking shape. Lincoln Heights, which was established in the 1830s on the bluffs around the Los Angeles River, is considered by many historians to be Los Angeles's first neighborhood, attracting many of the city's wealthiest residents. However, the community did not boom until 1889, when the Los Angeles Cable Railroad opened a short line that stretched across the river.

The 1830s additionally saw an influx of European settlers in Los Angeles, following in the footsteps of wealthy easterners such as Abel Stearns and Jonathan Temple, who moved to the area in the 1820s and came to control much of the region. Although not as sizable as the mass migrations that would bring people to the area in the later part of the nineteenth century, many of the people who moved to Los Angeles during this time went on to play integral roles in the city's development.

One of the most important settlers who arrived during this time was Jean-Louis Vignes, a French-born winemaker who arrived in Los Angeles in 1831. Vignes purchased 104 acres of land along the Los Angeles River near modern-day Alameda and Aliso Streets.

El Aliso Vineyard was named after an extremely old sycamore tree on the property. The tree itself, which sprouted sometime in the late fifteenth century, was a landmark and stood for more than four hundred years. Sixty feet tall and two hundred feet wide, the tree was a popular gathering spot for the city's earliest residents. A witness to much of the city's early development, the tree ultimately succumbed to urbanization in the 1890s, when the loss of topsoil and construction of nearby streets took their ultimate toll.

Vignes originally planted the land with Mission grapes like the ones that had been grown at nearby Mission San Gabriel since the late eighteenth century; however, dissatisfied with the wine that these grapes produced, he imported vines from the Bordeaux region of France. The process was incredibly difficult; reportedly, the roots of the vines were wrapped in moss and potato slices to help them survive the voyage.

By the mid-1830s, Vignes was producing Cabernet Franc and Sauvignon Blanc, making him both the earliest and most significant winemaker in California at the time. By 1840, Vignes had realized the Los Angeles market couldn't satisfy his supply, so he began shipping wine throughout the state. Within a few years, he was producing about 150,000 bottles per year, and

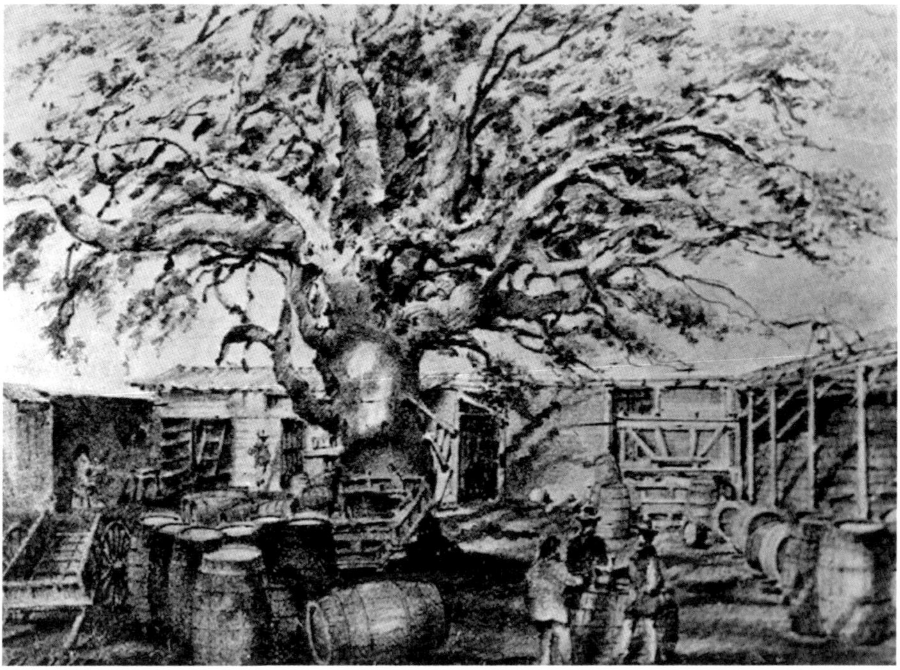

This drawing shows Jean-Louis Vignes's El Aliso Vineyard during the middle of the nineteenth century, including the namesake sycamore tree (*aliso*) itself. When the tree died in the 1890s, it was more than four hundred years old. Nearby Vignes Street still pays tribute to the winemaker's contributions to the city. *Courtesy the Los Angeles Public Library.*

his wine was being enjoyed by men such as William Tecumseh Sherman and President John Tyler.

Not limiting himself to wine, Vignes also was responsible for the first orange grove in Los Angeles (in 1834), as well as numerous other successful crops. By 1855, at the age of seventy-five, Vignes had sold El Aliso to his nephews for $40,000; for the last few years of his life, Vignes continued to be a civic leader, helping to finance a Catholic hospital and Los Angeles's first public school. At the time of his death in 1862, he was one of the most prominent men in the region.

As for the vineyard he had founded, his nephews sold it to German immigrants, who turned it into Los Angeles's first brewery. In the subsequent decades, the land that originally was home to Vignes's French vines was developed until his original plot of land was entirely unrecognizable; the only remnants of his legacy are Aliso Street, named after the famed sycamore tree, and Vignes Street, which approximately bisects his original plot of land.

Another notable local occurrence occurred in 1835, when gold was discovered in San Francisquito Canyon forty miles to the north of Los Angeles. Although completely eclipsed by the more famous gold rush in northern California thirteen years later, the area was mined until the turn of the twentieth century, and apparently small amounts of gold can still be found in undeveloped parts of the canyon.

There are several adobes in Los Angeles County that were built during the 1830s that are still standing. Perhaps the most notable is the Centinela Adobe, constructed in 1834 in what is today Inglewood. Built by Ygnacio Machado, the home was the seat of the twenty-five-thousand-acre Rancho Aguaje de la Centinela. Although threatened by demolition several times during its long history, the home is now used as a historic museum. The oldest part of the Andrés Pico Adobe (located in the San Fernando Valley) also dates from this same year.

The 1830s, as a whole, saw growing tensions in Los Angeles and the first stirrings of resistance to Mexican rule that would ultimately culminate in the Mexican-American War. It was, in many ways, the last decade in which Los Angeles still entirely resembled the Spanish pueblo that it was founded as; the war, several years later, would change the face of the city forever.

BEFORE THE WAR: LOS ANGELES, 1840–1845

In the years immediately before the Mexican-American War, Los Angeles continued to grow steadily, particularly with more eastern settlers. As the population rose, tensions also continued to grow, particularly between *Californios* (Roman Catholics of Spanish descent who lived in Alta California and had a very strong sense of independence) and Mexican rulers. Californios, for the most part, opposed Mexican-appointed governors, given their geographic isolation from Mexico. These tensions culminated in battle in the early months of 1845.

The Battle of Providencia took place in the San Fernando Valley north of Los Angeles, in what is now Burbank. Manuel Micheltorena, governor of Alta California, was disliked by many Californios, who quickly began to organize a revolt in November 1844. Several months later, on February 20, two hundred troops headed by former governor Juan Bautista Alvarez succeeded in expelling Micheltorena's equally sized army back to Mexico. Despite heavy fire from both sides, the only

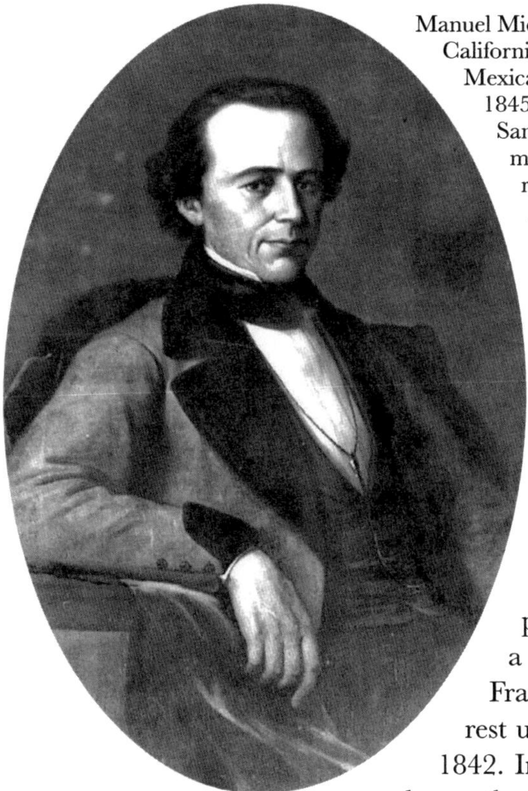

Manuel Micheltorena, governor of Alta California, played a critical role during the Mexican era of California's history. In 1845, at the Battle of Providencia (in the San Fernando Valley), Micheltorena's men were defeated by a band of revolutionaries led by Juan Bautista Alvarez. *Courtesy the University of California–Berkeley.*

casualty in the battle was a single animal (either a horse or a mule).

The early 1840s also saw the second discovery of gold in the Los Angeles area. In Placerita Canyon (part of Rancho San Francisco near present-day Santa Clarita), a young man by the name of Francisco Lopez stopped to take a rest under an oak tree on March 9, 1842. In his sleep, he allegedly had a dream that he was floating on a pool of gold. As the story goes, he awoke, pulled several wild onions from beneath the tree and found flakes of gold clinging to their roots. This romanticized story has been called into question by historians, who point out that Lopez had studied mineralogy in college, but regardless, his discovery sparked a minor gold rush that brought two thousand people from Mexico to the area. The tree where he made his discovery is preserved as the "Oak of the Golden Dream," California Historic Landmark #168, on the property of Placerita Canyon State Park.

The Los Cerritos Ranch House, located in present-day Long Beach, also dates to this time. Described by one historian as "the largest and most impressive adobe residence erected in southern California during the Mexican period," the home was built by Jonathan Temple in 1844. Temple, from Massachusetts, was one of the most prominent landowners in Los Angeles's earliest days. The home was used as the headquarters for his large cattle ranching operations.

Although it fell into disrepair after Temple's death, the home was completely refurbished in the early twentieth century; subsequently, the land was sold to the City of Long Beach for use as a museum. Today, the Cerritos Ranch House serves as a unique window into the Mexican era of Southern California's history.

The first half of the 1840s was the calm before the storm, before Los Angeles was torn apart by a deadly war. Pío Pico, who had formerly served as governor of Alta California in 1832, was reappointed to the position in 1845; during his tenure, he successfully made Los Angeles the capital of Alta California. However, despite strong rule by Mexican leaders, by the middle part of the decade it had become apparent that tensions throughout the Southwest United States were quickly making war inevitable.

THE MEXICAN-AMERICAN WAR IN LOS ANGELES

Following the annexation of Texas in 1845 and growing unrest in northern Mexican provinces, President James K. Polk declared war on Mexico on May 13, 1846 (for a complete history of the war's origins, see K. Jack Bauer's *The Mexican War, 1846–1848*). Throughout the war, much of the fighting was centered on California, as the region was politically, economically and socially important to both nations. However, while Northern California events (such as the Bear Flag Rebellion) are still fondly remembered to this day, much of Los Angeles's role in the war has been all but forgotten.

On July 7, 1846, U.S. naval forces successfully captured the town of Monterey with no opposition, effectively solidifying American rule of Northern California. Governor Pico, who had the only Californio troops available in the entire state, decided to center his resistance in Los Angeles alongside General José María Castro.

Following the capture of Monterrey, Commodore Robert F. Stockton captured the harbor of San Pedro and, several days later, led his men into Los Angeles on August 13. Stockton was followed shortly thereafter by General John C. Frémont and his famed California Battalion. The next several weeks were spent organizing a rudimentary civic government, and the city was left under the command of Captain Archibald H. Gillespie, Frémont's second in command.

Despite having been captured so easily, there still existed a very strong anti-American sentiment in Los Angeles at this time. Gillespie did nothing but exacerbate this hatred, and his 48 undisciplined troops were considered a nuisance by many of the city's 1,500 residents. Gillespie was well aware of rumors of a revolt, but tensions finally came to a head in the early hours of September 23, 1846.

At 3:00 a.m., twenty armed Californios attacked Gillespie's men in the Government House, an old adobe that was located on the northeast corner of Main and Temple Streets. Although no one was killed, in the days that followed, the Californios assembled under Captain José María Flores and prepared for a more organized resistance.

Meanwhile, Gillespie gathered what weapons and supplies he could from his headquarters at Government House. On the night of September 24, John Brown (more famously known as Juan Flaco) was able to escape Los Angeles undetected by the Californios and made a legendary ride to San Francisco in only four days, warning Commodore Stockton of the impending revolt and earning himself the nickname "the Paul Revere of California."

Several days later, Captain Gillespie and his troops left Government House under the cover of night and marched a quarter of a mile to Fort Hill (later renamed Fort Moore Hill), a position that was, theoretically, more defensible. However, Gillespie did not determine whether the hill had a source of water, and his men were forced to surrender the following day on account of his serious error.

The terms of the surrender allowed the soldiers to keep their small arms and safely return to San Pedro. While no lives were lost, the blow to the American cause was still overwhelming. Despite having complete control over the northern part of the state, Americans were unable to maintain possession of Southern California.

Several days later, after receiving word of the situation in Los Angeles from Juan Flaco, Captain William Mervine sailed into San Pedro and quickly planned a march to retake the city from the Californios. However, the weary American soldiers proved no match for the mounted Californios, who were both quicker and more effective with their fighting. This skirmish would come to be known as the Battle of Dominguez Rancho (now located in northern Long Beach) or the Battle of Old Woman's Gun, in reference to the Californios' sole piece of artillery, which had been hidden in an old woman's garden.

Ten Americans were wounded in the failed offensive, four of whom would later die from their injuries. These casualties were buried on Deadman's Island, one of two small islands located in San Pedro Harbor. Although Deadman's Island was dredged away in 1928, the other island—originally known as Rattlesnake Island—was renamed and developed into modern-day Terminal Island.

Further action to reclaim Los Angeles was postponed until the end of 1846. Commodore Stockton moved his troops south to San Diego in order to receive supplies and further training; while there, he was met by Brigadier General Stephen Watts Kearny. On December 28 and 29, these two men and their 607 troops traveled north out of San Diego along the present-day route of Highway 101.

Meanwhile, Frémont and his troops were traveling south from Monterey, also hoping to retake Los Angeles. Captain Flores assembled as many Californio troops as he could in anticipation for the American attacks. The stage was set for what would prove to be Los Angeles's largest battles of the war.

RIO SAN GABRIEL, LA MESA AND THE TREATY OF CAHUENGA

On January 8, 1847, Kearny and Stockton's troops reached the San Gabriel River and selected a location for their troops to cross. However, Commodore Stockton did not anticipate patches of quicksand or the water's quick current; the crossing was further complicated by Flores's position on the bluffs across the river. Flores himself was plagued by makeshift ammunition and undisciplined troops, and ultimately the American forces prevailed.

Having begun at 2:00 p.m., the battle was completed by 3:30 p.m. The Californio troops rallied to the battle cry of "Viva Los Californios!" while the Americans countered by shouting, "New Orleans! New Orleans!"—the Battle of Rio San Gabriel marked the thirty-first anniversary of Andrew Jackson's heroic victory during the War of 1812. By the end of the day, Flores, for whom defeat seemed inevitable, had moved all of his troops back to Los Angeles.

The site of the Battle of Rio San Gabriel is currently located in the cities of Whittier, Pico Rivera and Montebello. In 1945, almost a century after the battle took place, the site was dedicated as California State Historical Landmark #385. A plaque standing at the northeast corner of Washington Boulevard and Bluff Road in Montebello still commemorates the event.

On January 9, the following day, American troops advanced to Pio Pico's ranch in the hopes of finding the Californios there. Unsuccessful, they then marched across the plain between the San Gabriel River and Los Angeles. Along the way, they were met with Flores's remaining soldiers in what would be the last armed resistance in the state of California during the war.

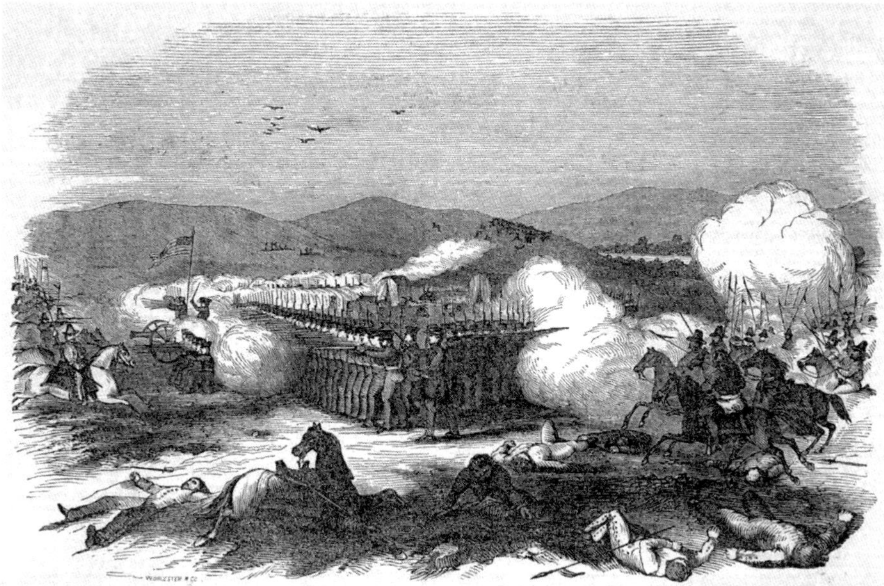

One of two major battles of the Mexican-American War fought around Los Angeles, the Battle of Rio San Gabriel (January 8, 1847) was a decisive victory for the American forces, who repeatedly shouted, "New Orleans!" in honor of the thirty-first anniversary of Jackson's heroic victory. *Courtesy the University of California–Berkeley.*

The Battle of La Mesa was a very one-sided engagement. Stockton's command of his troops dispersed the Californian artillery in a matter of minutes, and the American troops marched into Los Angeles shortly thereafter. Like the Rio San Gabriel battlefield, this site is currently a registered California State Historical Landmark (#167), and a plaque can be found at the intersection of Exchange Avenue and Downey Road in Vernon. Other plaques memorializing the battle can be found in front of Vernon City Hall.

The Americans, having finally reacquired Los Angeles, saw that a treaty was drafted in order to put an end to the fighting. John C. Frémont, who arrived several days after the fighting in Los Angeles had come to an end, met with Mexican governor Andrés Pico on January 13, 1847, in order to sign the document. José Antonio Carrillo, who had defeated the Americans at the Battle of Dominguez Rancho, drafted the treaty in both English and Spanish.

Because the meeting was held at Campo de Cahuenga, an adobe ranch house located in modern-day North Hollywood, the agreement came to be

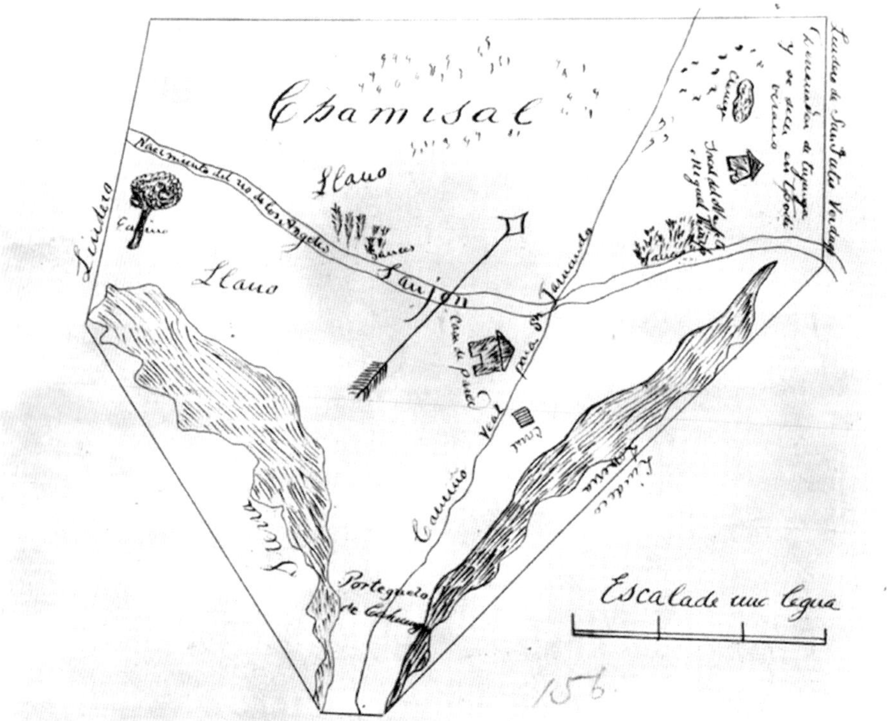

An early hand-drawn map shows the location of the adobe within Campo de Cahuenga, where the Treaty of Cahuenga was signed. Although not a formal treaty, the document put an end to fighting in Alta California. *Courtesy the Los Angeles Public Library.*

known as the "Treaty of Cahuenga." The ranch house where the treaty was actually signed was demolished in 1900, but the outline of the home and part of the original foundation are still preserved. The site is protected as a historic landmark on national, state and city levels and is currently run by the City of Los Angeles.

The treaty itself was fair to both sides, calling for both Americans and Californios to release all prisoners. So long as Californios obeyed the laws of the United States, they were allowed to return to their homes and were to be given the same rights as Americans. When the war ended the following year, many former enemies of the United States became citizens and went on to become very prominent residents of Los Angeles.

Following the conclusion of the fighting, American troops quickly set about working on a fort to protect the city from future attack. Located on the same hill where Gillespie had unsuccessfully moved his men the year

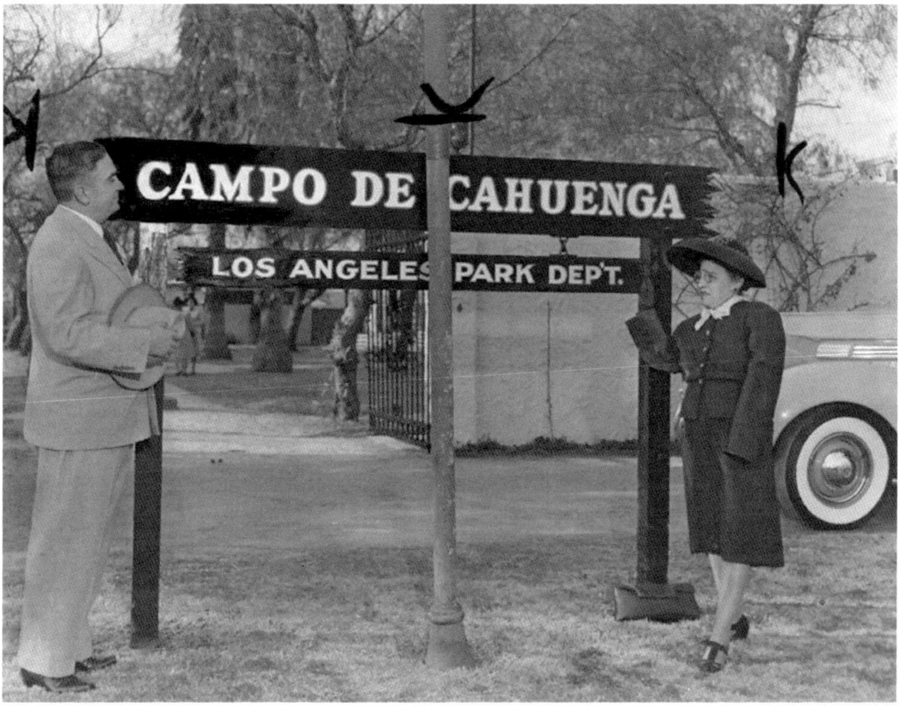

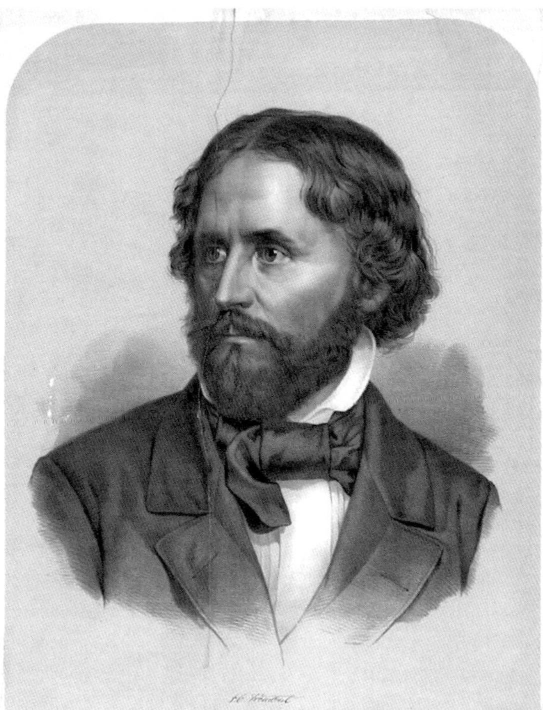

Above: City officials gather at Campo de Cahuenga in January 1947 to celebrate the 100th anniversary of the signing of the treaty. Today, the site is managed by the Los Angeles Parks Department, and the site of the original adobe is marked out in the parking lot. *Courtesy the Los Angeles Public Library.*

Right: Although he did not actually fire a shot in the campaign for Los Angeles, John C. Frémont was responsible for negotiating the Treaty of Cahuenga with Mexican general Andres Pico. Although once a household name in California, Frémont's legacy has largely been forgotten. *Courtesy the Library of Congress.*

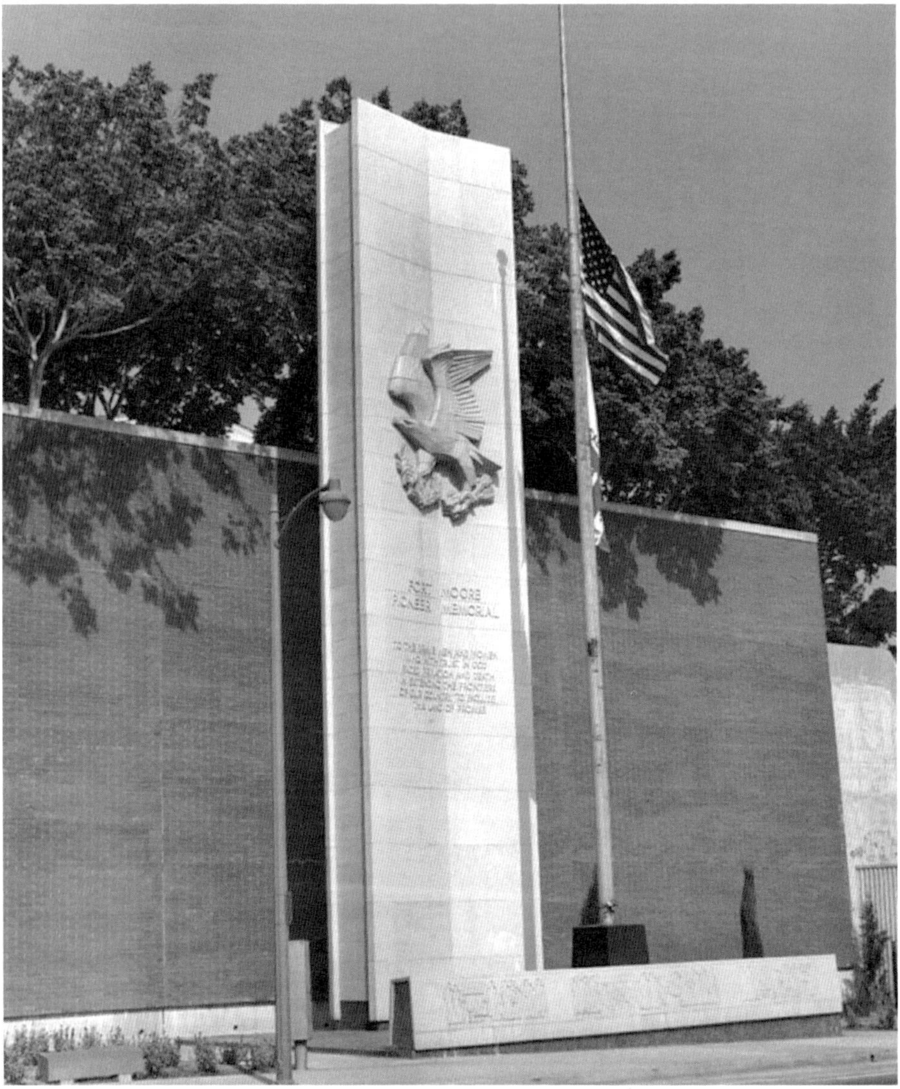

Dedicated in 1957, the Fort Moore Pioneer Memorial stands on the site of Fort Moore. A large bas-relief at the site depicts the Mormon Battalion raising an American flag on Los Angeles's first Independence Day in 1847. *Courtesy the Los Angeles Public Library.*

before, Fort Moore (as it came to be known) was constructed in large part by the Mormon Battalion—famous for being the only religious military unit in American history.

The fort itself was never completed and, due to the end of the war, was abandoned by 1849. Four years later, the site was razed and turned into a public playground. This site, still known as Fort Moore Hill, continued to play a critical role in the rest of the story of Victorian Los Angeles.

In 1957, the Fort Moore Pioneer Monument was created on the east side of the former fort (located on the southwest corner of Hill Street and Cesar Chavez Avenue). The highlight of the monument is a seventy-eight- by forty-three-foot terra-cotta bas-relief depicting the Mormon Battalion hoisting the American flag over Los Angeles for the city's first Independence Day celebration in 1847. A sixty-eight-foot pylon stands nearby. Originally, the site was also home to an eighty-foot waterfall, which was turned off due to a 1977 drought and has never been restored. Recently, there has been a movement to refurbish the monument to its original glory.

The period between the beginning of the Victorian era and the end of Mexican rule in Los Angeles was transformative for the city. Its relative isolation helped to mark Los Angeles as a lawless, western town—a reputation that would continue to grow as the city began to expand rapidly in the mid-nineteenth century. Many streets and neighborhoods that still exist today were established during this time, and several adobes that are still standing help to give modern residents and visitors a glimpse of what life was like during the city's very early Victorian period. With the closing of the Mexican-American War also came the end of the Mexican way of life in Southern California; as the decades progressed, the city became increasingly westernized as the metropolis that exists today began to take shape.

Chapter 2

Independence and Incorporation, 1849–1869

A Wild West Town

The time immediately following the war proved incredibly consequential for the small town of Los Angeles. Now under American rule, it was determined that the city's land had to be surveyed and sold in an American manner; the Spanish and Mexican concepts of landownership did not carry over into this new system.

A small real estate boom was created, with many of the city's most wealthy and prominent residents purchasing land on the outskirts of town. From that point on, lower-income residents and minorities were typically confined to the heart of the former pueblo, which had historically been the home of wealthy individuals. This trend would continue to plague Los Angeles for much of its history.

While the California Gold Rush of 1849 was located in the northern part of the state, the event also had a profound impact on Los Angeles. With the large influx of people to the north came a new demand for food and supplies, which the southland was more than happy to meet. Los Angeles County quickly began producing more beef than any other county in the state, which resulted in large economic growth.

Furthermore, many hopeful gold miners who took southern routes into the state were so enchanted with Los Angeles that they never actually made it to the Sierras; likewise, many who had tried their luck and failed in the gold business eventually settled in Los Angeles. Between 1850 and 1860, the city nearly tripled in size.

Another consequence of the California Gold Rush was a large influx of Mexican citizens from the northern state of Sonora hoping to strike it rich in America. These immigrants, who introduced the method of panning for gold to California, experienced animosity from many Americans who harbored resentment from the Mexican-American War only a few years earlier. Due to this, many Sonorans were driven from their mines in the Sierras and relocated to Los Angeles upon their return trip to Mexico.

This large population influx resulted in the establishment of one of Los Angeles's first ethnic barrios: Sonoratown. Although by no means the only one of its kind (many other cities also had "Sonoratowns"), Los Angeles's was unique in its size and longevity. The neighborhood sprung up in the area immediately north of the Plaza, where many neglected adobes were still standing from the city's earlier days.

Sonoratown was, in many ways, the last vestige of what life was like under Spanish and Mexican rule. As the rest of the city developed at breakneck speed, Sonoratown's residents continued to live their lives as Los Angeles residents had for generations. Many tourists visited the barrio to see what life had been like in the past; the irony is that despite the old-fashioned way of life, the neighborhood was established after California had already come under United States rule.

Eventually, around the turn of the twentieth century, industrialization made the property valuable, and Sonoratown began to disappear. By the 1930s, the area had become Los Angeles's new Chinatown, and nearby Olvera Street was transformed into the hub of Mexican culture. Although no trace of the settlement exists today, Sonoratown was an integral part of Los Angeles for half a century.

The 1850 census (Los Angeles's first) registered 1,610 people living in the city. Going through the list of names, a vast majority of residents listed professions such as laborer, farmer or grazier—showing how rural the city still was. A large percentage of the population was still composed of foreign-born immigrants, both from Mexico and Europe. However, as California quickly progressed toward statehood, Los Angeles stayed on the cutting edge of development.

The county of Los Angeles was established in February 18, 1850, as one of California's twenty-seven original counties. At first, it included parts of what are today Orange, San Bernardino, Riverside and Kern Counties, although it would vastly shrink over the next half century. At that time, there were no incorporated cities anywhere in the county, although due to its sizable population, the city of Los Angeles was the obvious choice for county seat.

Only a month and a half after the county was established, the city of Los Angeles itself was incorporated on April 4. It is interesting to note that the state of California was not admitted to the United States until a little more than five months later. A civic government was established in July 1850, and over the next few years, many of the civil services associated with a city were established.

During the 1850s, Los Angeles had a terrible reputation as a lawless, dangerous town. Many sources claim that, on average, there was a homicide for every day of the year in the city. While these numbers may be somewhat inflated, it is truly startling to think of a city with a population of under two thousand experiencing hundreds of murders each year. Alongside the murders, Los Angeles also suffered from a number of gambling halls, brothels, saloons and other establishments of ill repute.

Homicides were not the only killings that plagued Los Angeles—from the 1850s through the 1880s, the city was the site of dozens of public lynchings and legal executions. Due to Los Angeles's isolated nature and violent reputation at this time, many local citizens sought to take the law into their own hands, leading to the large number of public killings. More recent scholars, however, have often questioned whether the accused were actually guilty of any crimes or were merely scapegoats and victims of racial hatred.

Los Angeles attempted to take precautions against the rampant lawlessness, usually to no avail. When the city was incorporated in 1850, there was both a city marshal and a county sheriff, although these offices had a hard time keeping up with the vast amount of crime; within a few years, most locals thought it better to take the law into their own hands than to trust the ineffective authority.

Tensions came to a head in 1853, when City Marshal Jack Whaling was shot to death by a bounty hunter. A group of volunteers, led by Dr. A.W. Hope, formed the "Los Angeles Rangers"—the city's first police force. The Rangers wore white ribbons that read, "City Police—Authorized by the Council of Los Angeles," in lieu of a uniform. The Rangers only lasted a few years; they were replaced by the "Los Angeles City Guards" in 1855, who were the first police officers to wear official uniforms.

These early police forces were practically as ineffective as the marshal and sheriff, and crime rates continued to skyrocket. Indeed, the police themselves were responsible for more than a few lynchings and unjust imprisonments. One incredible anecdote shows just how primitive the criminal justice system was in describing the state of the county jail in the mid-1850s: because the jail lacked cells, criminals were simply chained to giant logs in the prison yard to keep them from escaping.

The first official police force in Los Angeles didn't arrive until 1869, when the city hired six officers. In the early days, these policemen not only had to go after criminals but also served as dog catchers and tax collectors. Today, the Los Angeles Police Department operates on a $1.4 billion budget and employs more than thirteen thousand individuals; in 1869, the force was given only $50 to furnish its headquarters.

A TIME OF FIRSTS

Despite the social ills present in Los Angeles during this time (and there were many), the city was also making large strides toward modernization. The 1850s saw several landmark occurrences that proved that Los Angeles was well on its way to becoming a cultural hub. Statehood in 1850 brought an increasing number of new settlers to California, with a large number of them settling in the Los Angeles area. People of different races and religions were soon contributing to local politics and shaping the face of the city.

One of the first necessities to be addressed was the issue of public schools. While sporadic schooling had been offered in Los Angeles under Spanish and Mexican rule and a school district had been established in 1852, it wasn't until March 19, 1855, that the first public schoolhouse in Los Angeles would be opened. Located at the northwest corner of Spring Street and Second Street, the brick building consisted of four rooms and cost $6,000 to construct. Around the same time this school was built, an identical structure was built on Bath Street (now North Main Street).

Although in the heart of downtown today, residents at the time complained that the school was "on the edge of town" and inconvenient for their children. Despite this, the school continued to serve the city until 1884, when a short-lived city hall was built on the site (today, an annex of the Los Angeles Times Building occupies the corner). A small plaque remembers all of the prior buildings that stood on the site.

One humorous, and perhaps apocryphal, anecdote about the city's first schoolhouse demonstrates just how primitive the city was in the mid-nineteenth century. A young teacher thought it would be beneficial for there to be trees on the school's property to provide the students with shade; however, he didn't anticipate the subsequent influx of squirrels that his trees brought. Undeterred, he purchased a gun and would shoot at the squirrels between his students' recitations.

Today, the Los Angeles Unified School District serves 640,000 students and is the second-largest employer in the county; it is incredible to realize that the second-largest school district in the nation can trace its history back to two humble brick buildings located on opposite sites of the embryonic city.

In addition to the city's first schoolhouse, the rest of the 1850s reads like a laundry list of historic "firsts" in the city. Los Angeles's first newspaper published its debut issue on May 17, 1851. Because it published two pages in English and two in Spanish, it was called both the *Los Angeles Star* and *La Estrella*. The *Star*, which often took a very radical perspective (particularly during the Civil War, when it espoused slavery and vilified President Lincoln), was published until 1879 (with a break between 1864 and 1868). However, by that time, the newspaper business had become more crowded; the *Evening Express* and the *Evening Herald* began in 1871 and 1873, respectively. Two years later, in 1881, the *Los Angeles Times* was founded.

In 1853, the city and county worked together to build Los Angeles County's first public building: a jail on the northwest corner of Spring and Franklin Streets. Although Spring has been rerouted and Franklin no longer exists, the site of this historic building would have been approximately located near the southwest corner of the current city hall.

The mid-1850s also saw the expansion of Los Angeles's cultural and religious heritage with the founding of the Hebrew Benevolent Society—not only the city's first organized Jewish community but also Los Angeles's first formal charitable organization. In 1855, the Hebrew Benevolent Society Cemetery was founded in Chavez Ravine; although the interred bodies were relocated in 1910, the site is recognized as California Historical Landmark #822. Designated as the "First Jewish Site in Los Angeles," a plaque is located at Lookout Drive and Lilac Terrace (just south of Dodger Stadium).

As anyone with a familiarity of the region's history knows, water (or the lack thereof) has plagued Los Angeles since its earliest days. For much of the city's early history, the "Zanja Madre" (or "Mother Ditch") carried water from the Los Angeles River to the Plaza and elsewhere. In 1857, Judge William Dryden founded the Los Angeles Water Works (the first water company in the area) in an attempt to improve the rudimentary system that was in place. Near Solano Canyon, Dryden constructed a forty-foot water wheel to bring water from the Zanja Madre to central reservoir in the Plaza;

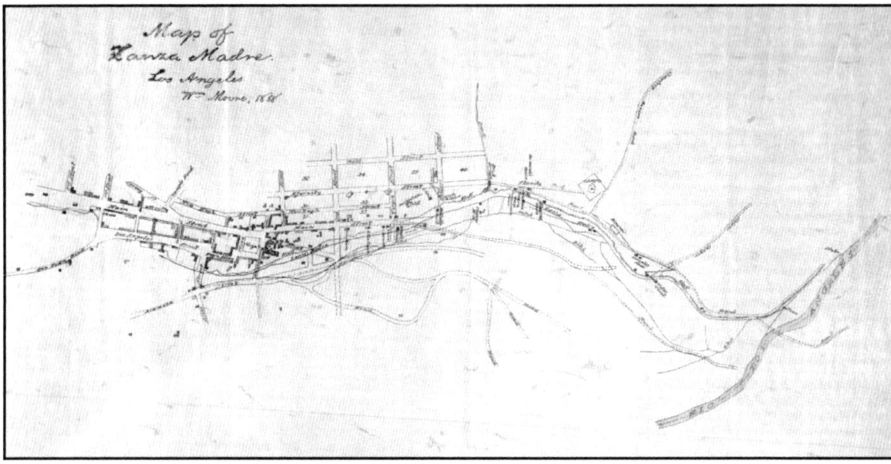

The Zanja Madre ("Mother Ditch") was Los Angeles's first attempt at a waterworks system, delivering water from the Los Angeles River by way of a series of small canals. This map from 1888 shows the extent of the Zanja throughout downtown. *Courtesy Water and Power Associates.*

from there, it would be distributed to the city via underground wooden pipes. A fragile system from the start, within four or five years Dryden's operations had ceased due to flooding that destroyed much of his infrastructure. Over the next few years, others would unsuccessfully attempt similar setups, but it would be decades until a massive overhaul of Los Angeles's water problem was undertaken.

The year 1859 saw Los Angeles's first attempt at founding a public library, when several prominent city fathers gathered to establish a reading room. Through donations, a "motley collection of volumes" was assembled, but the one-dollar monthly fee proved too costly for the business model to be successful. The books that had been collected were later auctioned off to cover the debt of the failed social experiment, and it would be more than a decade later before another attempt was made.

WAR (ALMOST) RETURNS TO LOS ANGELES

The Mexican-American War wasn't the only national conflict to have affected Los Angeles. Although nearly all of the fighting was centered thousands of miles away, the American Civil War still brought troops and forts to the state of California. A large number of immigrants to the Los Angeles area in the decade after statehood were from the Southeast, and many prominent locals were afraid of a secessionist movement taking hold. One such resident was Phineas Banning, who personally wrote a letter to President Abraham Lincoln urging him to tighten the Union's grip on California for fear of losing the state.

As a preventative measure, the Union army moved troops from Fort Tejon, north of Los Angeles in the Grapevine, to the newly established Camp Latham. Located in what is today Culver City near the intersection of Overland and Jefferson Boulevards, Camp Latham proved to be very short-lived; in 1861, Banning (alongside Los Angeles's second mayor, Benjamin Davis Wilson) donated land for the construction of a more proper camp. Named Camp Drum after Colonel Richard Coulter Drum, by early 1862 all troops had moved from Camp Latham. Over the next few years, twenty-two buildings would be constructed on the property.

During the course of the Civil War, between 2,000 and 7,000 soldiers were stationed at Camp Drum; by comparison, the 1860 census lists the population of Los Angeles as only 4,385. Although there were no battles in California, Los Angeles–area troops did march from Camp Drum to Picacho Peak, Arizona, in 1862 for what would be the westernmost battle of the war. Following the Confederates' surrender in 1865, Fort Drum stayed

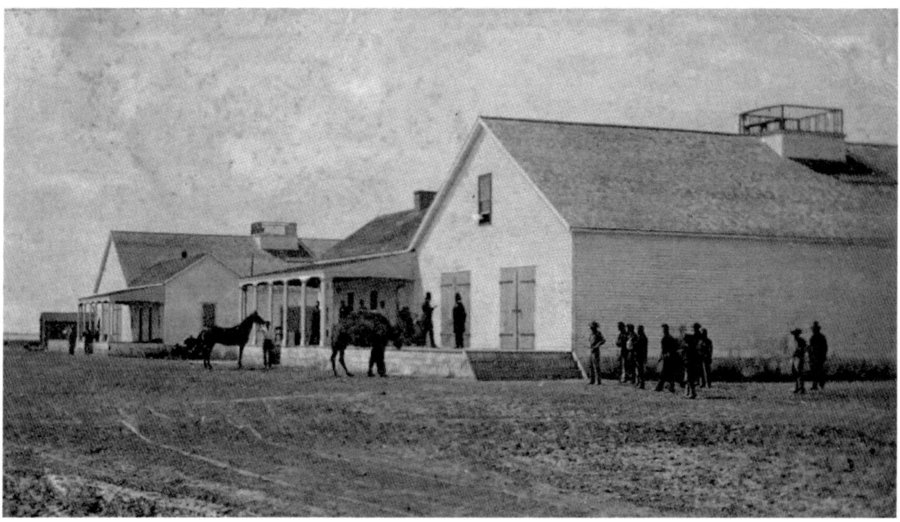

This picture, taken at Drum Barracks in 1863, is the only known photograph of the United States Camel Corps, a short-lived military program that attempted to use camels to carry supplies. Today, Drum Barracks is the only remnant of the Civil War in Los Angeles County. *Courtesy the Drum Barracks Garrison and Society.*

operational until the early 1870s as a deterrent in the Indian Wars. It was also toward the end of the Civil War that Camp Drum was renamed Drum Barracks, the name it retains today.

Following a preservation battle that can trace its roots back to the 1920s, two original structures from Camp Drum are still standing today—the only such sites in the Los Angeles area. The Drum Barracks Civil War Museum, located at 1052 North Banning Boulevard in Wilmington, occupies the junior officers' quarters. Open to the public for tours, the museum commemorates the site's history as the Union army headquarters in Southern California with numerous artifacts and costumed reenactors.

Located on the opposite corner of the same block (561 East Opp Street) is one of Camp Drum's powder magazines, used to store gunpowder during the war. Although vacant and in disrepair, recent preservation efforts have been underway to ensure that the structure is properly protected.

St. Vincent's College

In 1865, only a decade after Los Angeles constructed its first schoolhouse, the first college was founded in Southern California. Bishop Thaddeus Amat, who recognized the potential of Los Angeles as a major city (especially as Monterrey was losing significance), was a member of the Vincentian Order. Determined to spread the Catholic Church on the West Coast while also promoting higher education, Bishop Amat commissioned the founding of St. Vincent's College.

Originally, the school was based in the Don Vicente Lugo Adobe, one of the city's only two-story adobe structures. Demolished in 1951, the Lugo Adobe was situated east of the Plaza in what is now Father Junipero Serra Park. After only two years at this location, however, work began on the construction of a more traditional campus. The block bordered by Sixth, Seventh, Hill and Broadway became home to the new school; while not a large building, the stately Victorian architecture of St. Vincent's was nonetheless impressive for the still embryonic Los Angeles.

St. Vincent's was perpetually on the move, it seemed. The building that began serving students in 1868 would only last until 1887, when the college moved south to the intersection of Grand Avenue and Washington Boulevard (the site is now the parking lot for Olympic Auditorium). Once St. Vincent's moved out of its former campus, the U.S. Army occupied the

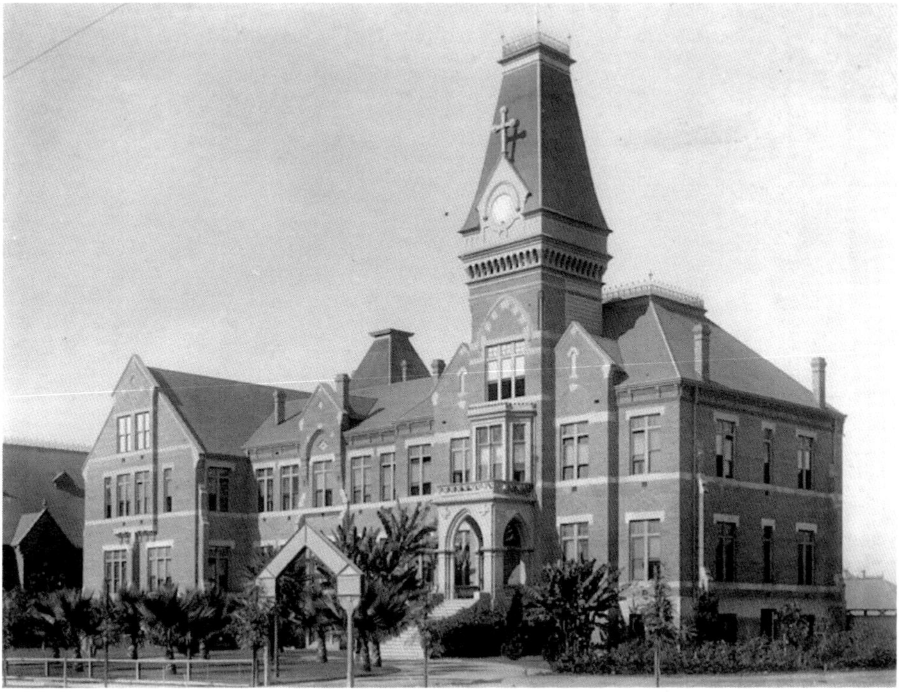

The Grand Avenue campus of St. Vincent's college featured striking Collegiate Gothic architecture, including a large mansard-roofed bell tower. However, this building existed for a relatively brief time before the ever-moving St. Vincent's College found a new home several miles away. *Courtesy the Los Angeles Public Library.*

site for a period of time; what had once been athletic fields became artillery training grounds.

The architecture of the former St. Vincent's campus was stunningly outdone at the new Grand Avenue location. The main college building was designed in a uniquely Victorian Collegiate Gothic style that ranks among the most impressive educational buildings in Los Angeles's history. However, despite the school's glowing reviews in contemporary newspapers (both the facilities and quality of education were praised), the school never generated much revenue, and by 1910, the Vincentians had turned control of the college over to the Jesuits.

Traces of the original St. Vincent's College downtown still persist to this day. Nearby where the school once sat is the St. Vincent Jewelry Center, named after St. Vincent Place—a small alley that bisects the block from north to south. Now home to many small restaurants and shops, St. Vincent Place can trace its origins back to when it was merely a walkway leading from the street to the college.

Today, the heritage of St. Vincent's College can be traced to both Loyola High School and Loyola Marymount University, both of which are descendants of Southern California's first college. Although as few as five hundred students ever graduated from St. Vincent's, it is undoubtedly a testament to the cultural growth that Los Angeles underwent during the 1860s.

PERSHING SQUARE PARK

Although the face of downtown Los Angeles has changed immeasurably since the 1860s, there is one feature that has been consistent for nearly 150 years. In 1866, Mayor Cristobal Aguilar set aside a square block of land as "La Plaza Abaja"—the lower plaza. Today, this same plot of land (bordered by Fifth, Sixth, Hill and Olive Streets) is known as Pershing Square Park and is the city's oldest public park.

Since its inception in 1866, Pershing Square has gone through numerous redevelopments and name changes. Early in its existence, ranchers used the

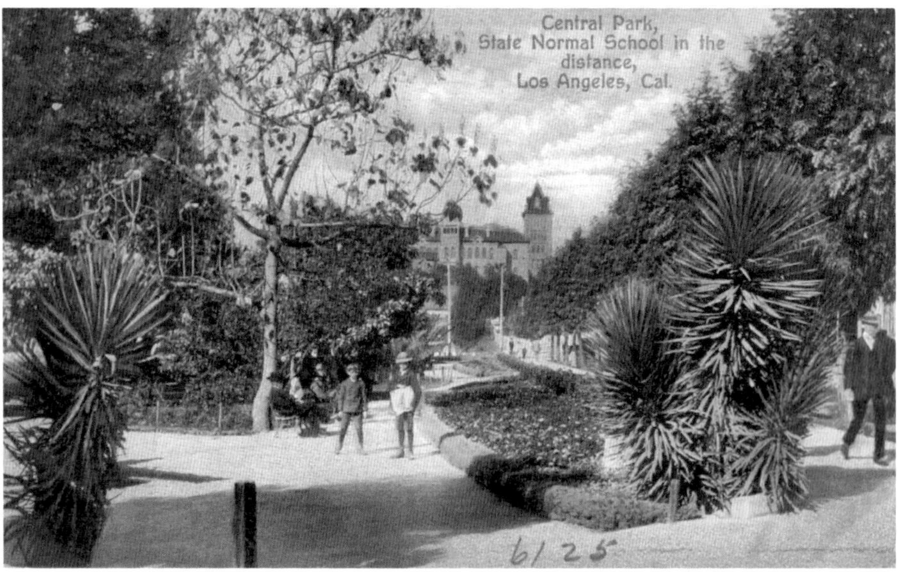

An early view of Pershing Square Park, when it was still known as Central Park (the State Normal School can be seen in the distance). Although considerably changed after numerous redevelopments during the twentieth century, Pershing Square—or, as it was once known, Central Park—is the city's oldest public park. *Courtesy Loyola Marymount University.*

common to graze their cattle, and it wasn't until 1870 that the city would set aside a budget for landscaping and rename the land Los Angeles Park. In 1886, a bandstand was added, and a massive renovation in 1910 was overseen by famed Los Angeles architect John Parkinson. Various names were used for the park over the years, but the most common proved to be Central Park. The current name, after General John "Black Jack" Pershing, would be given in the immediate aftermath of World War I in 1918.

Over the first half of the twentieth century, the park began to fall into disrepair, and in the early 1950s, the land was excavated for underground parking. The current park, which dates back to the mid-1990s, features modern sculptures that are a far cry from the park's earlier iterations. While little semblance of an actual park exists today, the site is still historic for the role it played in the city's early history; while skyscrapers were springing up across downtown, Central Park provided residents with some open space (even if only a square block).

One holdover from the park's late Victorian days is a statue of a Spanish-American War soldier dating to 1900. Sculpted by Samuel M. Goddard and dedicated to the Seventh California Infantry, this is the oldest piece of public artwork in the entire city.

PHINEAS BANNING AND SAN PEDRO

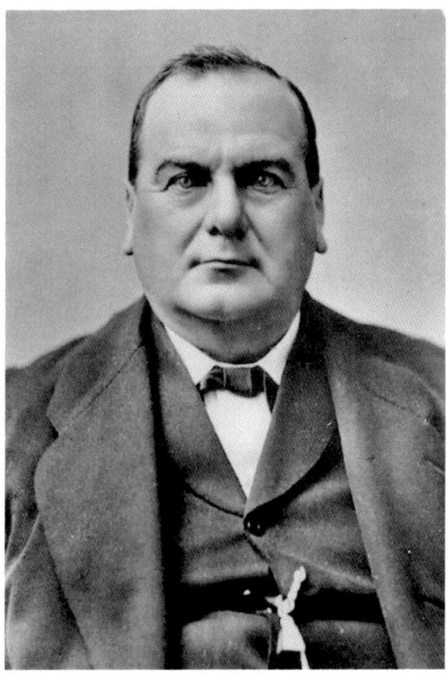

Few men were as influential in the development of Los Angeles as Phineas Banning. Banning established the first stagecoach and railroad lines from Los Angeles to San Pedro, where he developed a successful shipping harbor. Wilmington, where he lived, is named after his birthplace in Delaware. *Courtesy the Los Angeles Public Library.*

During the middle of the nineteenth century, few men did more to change the face of the Los Angeles area than Phineas Banning. Born in Delaware, Banning moved to Southern California when he was twenty-one years old; within a year of his arrival, he had established the first stagecoach line between the port of San Pedro and downtown Los Angeles. Within a few years, Banning and his partner, D.W. Alexander, were running stagecoaches up the coast to Ventura, Santa Barbara and San Luis Obispo; within a decade, the lines reached as far as Salt Lake City, Utah, and Yuma, Arizona.

Perhaps more important than his stagecoach lines was the potential that Banning saw in the Port of San Pedro. Although Richard Henry Dana Jr. described it as the worst harbor he had seen on his 1835 journey along the California coast, there were few alternatives in the area. Although Santa Monica would briefly be a contender for Los Angeles's shipping business decades later, there was little doubt of San Pedro's dominance, despite its geographical shortcomings.

The first steamer to dock in San Pedro was the *Gold Hunter* in 1849 while on its way from San Francisco to Mazatlan, and by the early 1850s, San Pedro had become a regular stop for steamers traveling up and down the coast. Determined to capitalize on this and turn San Pedro into a major shipping port, Banning and a group of investors purchased 640 acres next to the harbor in 1858. The docks and wharf that he constructed became known as "Banning's Landing" and were instrumental in bringing more shipping business to the port than ever before.

Banning initially named his new land New San Pedro; however, by 1863, he had changed the name to Wilmington, after his birthplace in Delaware. Today, the city of Wilmington still occupies much of Banning's original purchase from 1858.

The successful stagecoach line and shipping harbor were not enough for Phineas Banning, though; in 1869, he would again make history by establishing Southern California's first railroad. Banning was not the first person to attempt a rail line between San Pedro and Los Angeles; he would, however, become the first to receive support from the state, county and city governments. As a state senator, he proposed a bill that would authorize $150,000 in county stocks and $75,000 in city stocks to fund his railroad; the bill passed the legislature and was signed by Governor Henry Huntly Haight in early 1868.

Although he had political support, Banning still needed the public's support on his endeavor. Many people in Southern California, particularly in rural areas, were opposed to a railroad. In a strange breach of protocol, official precincts for the county's vote on the issue were never formally tallied; what ultimately tipped the scale was overwhelming support from both the communities of Wilmington and Los Angeles. Banning and his

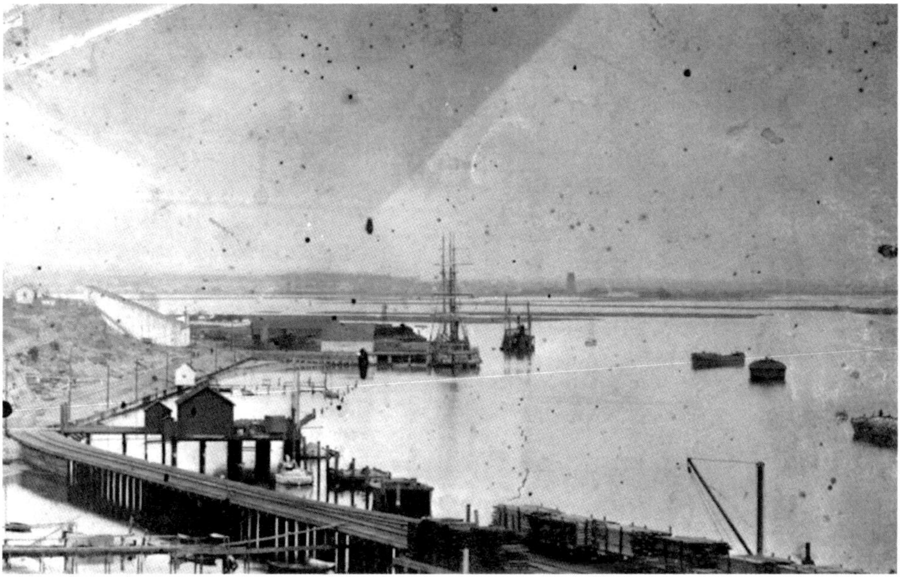

This photograph shows San Pedro Harbor in 1881, long before a breakwater would be constructed to protect the port from the elements. At this time, there was still competition between San Pedro and Santa Monica for Los Angeles's shipping business. *Courtesy the Los Angeles Public Library.*

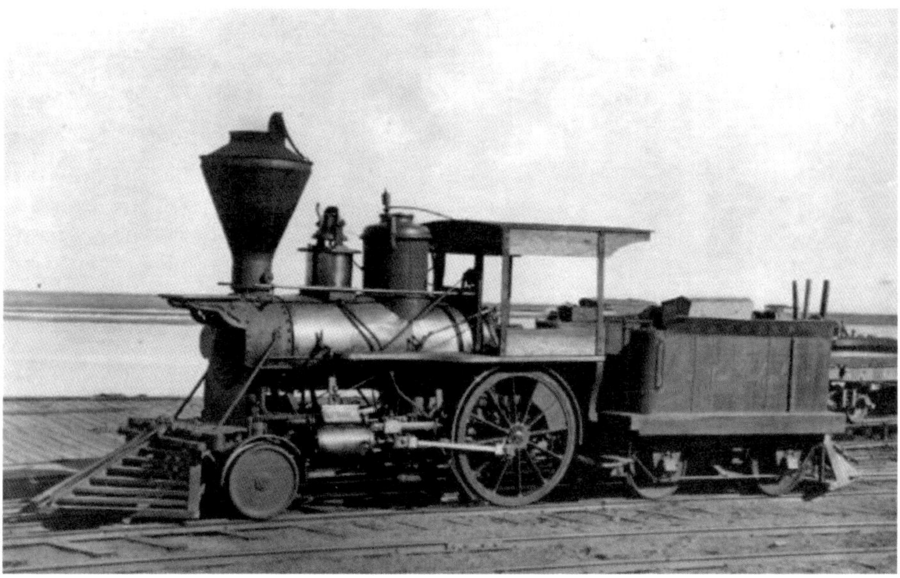

The San Gabriel, the first locomotive that served the Los Angeles & San Pedro Railroad, Southern California's first. The line was quickly acquired by the Southern Pacific Railroad, and the right-of-way still exists today as the Alameda Corridor. *Courtesy the Los Angeles Public Library.*

stagecoach business partner, D.W. Alexander, were awarded the contract for the construction of the line.

Work on the railroad progressed faster than expected through the end of 1868 and most of 1869, and a grand opening celebration was held on October 26, 1869 (two months ahead of schedule). About 1,500 people showed up to the line's depot on the southwest corner of Alameda and Commercial Streets to celebrate. Regular train service began several days later on November 1; cargo cost $6.00 per ton to ship, while a passenger could buy a one-way ticket from Los Angeles to Wilmington for $1.50 (to continue from Wilmington to the harbor was an additional $1.00).

The first locomotive to run on the Los Angeles & San Pedro Railroad was the San Gabriel, a small and oftentimes unreliable locomotive. Reports of the line's earliest days describe the train as breaking down every few days. After serving the line for a little more than five years, the San Gabriel was wrecked during a test run in January 1875 and was subsequently scrapped the following year.

The Los Angeles & San Pedro had an incredible effect on connecting Los Angeles to global markets. The amount of cargo that passed through the port more than doubled during the railroad's first two years, and after the line was acquired by the Southern Pacific in 1873, it played an important role in its decision to terminate the transcontinental railroad in Los Angeles and not San Diego.

Although the line's original depots and track are long gone, the route Banning laid out for the Los Angeles & San Pedro Railroad still connects downtown with the port. Running along the length of Alameda Street (which becomes State Route 47), the right-of-way was developed into the Alameda Corridor "expressway" over the past two decades. Although the Southern Pacific Railroad no longer exists and the track primarily runs below ground, the route of the Los Angeles & San Pedro still serves as a reminder of Los Angeles's entrance to the global economy.

One important trace of Phineas Banning's legacy in Wilmington is still standing. The Banning House, located at 401 East M Street, was constructed in 1864. Designed by Phineas himself, it has been described as the "finest example of domestic Greek Revival architecture in Southern California," at a time when the vast majority of buildings in the area were adobes. Until his untimely death in 1885, Banning used the house to host parties with government officials, civic leaders and other prominent men and women, and it became one of the first social hubs in the region.

The Banning family lived in the twenty-three-room home until 1925, and two years later, the twenty-acre property was transferred to the City of Los Angeles. Today, thanks to a preservation group spearheaded by Phineas's great-granddaughter, the entire property is open to the public as a "living history" museum. The house itself is open for tours, and visitors can also wander Banning's carriage house and gardens. Registered as a city, state and national landmark, the Banning House is arguably the best place in the entire county to be immersed in Victorian culture and everyday life.

The period from 1849 to 1869 saw Los Angeles gain its footing as an American city. Obviously, the abrupt transition from Spanish rule to Mexican rule to American rule over the course of only a few decades meant that Los Angeles would always have a unique culture blending the influence of all three powers. However, the 1850s and 1860s did see a marked shift away from the rancho system that had been predominant in Los Angeles for so long, as well as the rise of establishments such as higher education, public parks and newspapers, all of which had been more or less absent in Mexican California. Although far from becoming a truly American city, the seeds were sown for what was to come later in the decade.

CHAPTER 3

DEVELOPMENT OF THE CITY, 1870–1884

A RAPIDLY CHANGING CITY

Although Los Angeles made important strides toward becoming a major city during the 1850s and '60s, it still retained much of the character of the Wild West town it began as. Civic infrastructure was still lacking, and immigration to Los Angeles was still minimal—between 1860 and 1870, the city's population had only increased from about 4,400 people to 5,700 people. Despite California's admittance into the United States twenty years earlier, Los Angeles still appeared very much as it did under Mexican rule.

During the 1870s, things began to change. In large part due to the completion of the transcontinental railroad in 1869, the population would nearly double by the end of the decade, peaking at 11,183 in 1880. For the first time, substantial buildings were constructed downtown—hotels, business blocks and churches—that worked to give Los Angeles the appearance of a modern city. Education, at all levels, began to flourish as new institutions were founded, architects with distinctive styles began to rise in prominence and different religious traditions began to take hold in the fledgling city.

Although the city was far from the metropolis it would eventually become, the 1870s and early 1880s can be looked at as Los Angeles's "coming of age." No longer the adolescent town of the early American period, the city experienced a significant rise in prominence on a national scale and, by the

1880s, was poised to reach new heights. Although still marred by lawlessness, much of it racially based, the period from 1870 to 1884 was integral to the city's eventual ascendance to greatness.

PICO HOUSE

Pio Pico, who served as the last Mexican governor of California before the state achieved independence, remained a prominent citizen after he returned to Los Angeles following the Mexican-American War. In 1869, after becoming one of the wealthiest men in the region, he undertook an endeavor to open Los Angeles's first grand hotel: the Pico House.

When construction began on September 18, 1869, Los Angeles did not have any three-story buildings, and the existing hotels in the city were

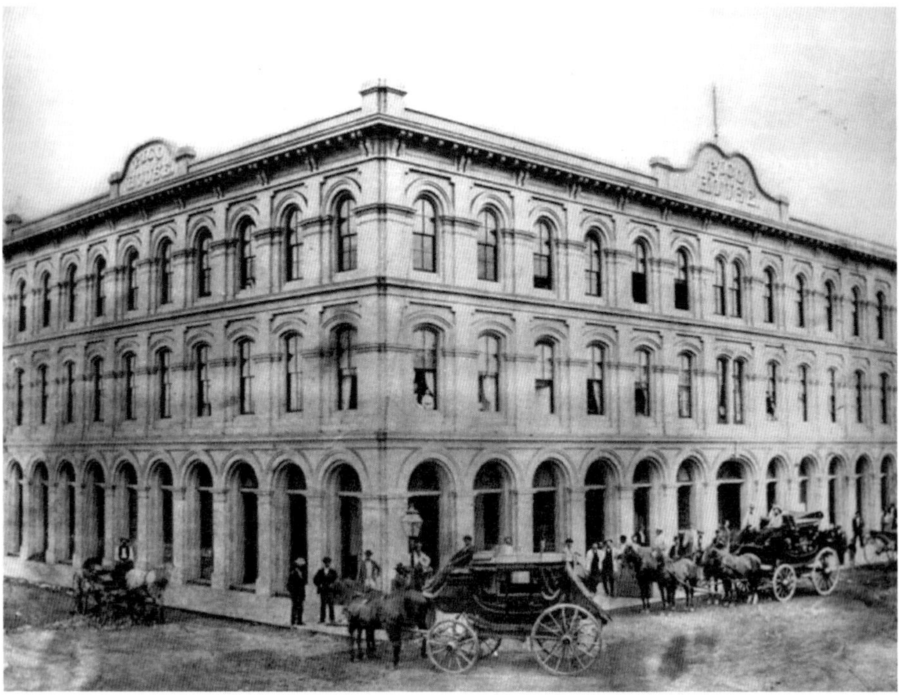

One of Los Angeles's first prominent buildings was the Pico House, an Italianate hotel constructed between 1869 and 1870 by Pio Pico. The Pico House is still standing today and is one of Los Angeles's most important remaining Victorian buildings. *Courtesy the Los Angeles Public Library.*

typically small and outdated. Pio Pico's vision for a lavish hotel was one of the first steps taken toward making Los Angeles a truly metropolitan city. The Pico House first opened its doors to the public less than a year later on June 9, 1870.

The building's architecture, which was designed by Ezra F. Kysor (Los Angeles's only prominent architect at the time, arguably), was inspired by the Italianate style. Before Mission and Spanish Colonial Revival architecture took hold of Southern California in the early twentieth century, European influences such as this were common. To this day, the building retains remarkable architectural integrity, and it's a hallmark of the Victorian era in Los Angeles.

Pico did not own his hotel for long, and by the 1880s, the core of downtown Los Angeles had begun to shift to the south, although the hotel remained incredibly popular until the turn of the twentieth century. After being used for decades as a boardinghouse, the property was acquired by the state in 1953. After undergoing extensive renovation during the 1980s and 1990s, the Pico House is now part of El Pueblo de Los Angeles State Historic Monument.

THE CHINESE MASSACRE

Perhaps the darkest chapter in Los Angeles's long and complex history came on October 24, 1871, in the form of the Chinese Massacre. One writer described the event as "one of the most bloody and barbarous tragedies in the annals of this State." To fully understand the event, though, some background information on Los Angeles during the 1870s is necessary. Located approximately where Los Angeles Street runs today, immediately south of the Plaza, was a street known as "Calle de los Negros" (named by Europeans after the dark-skinned Californios who populated the block). Although a shocking name by modern standards, Calle de los Negros was a staple on maps of Los Angeles for decades.

Calle de los Negros had a reputation for lawlessness; early historians describe the street as being lined with brothels, gambling houses and bars, and violent crimes were a regular activity. By the 1860s, Calle de los Negros had become the home of Los Angeles's first Chinatown, as some of the first Asian immigrants to the area had begun arriving. Tragedy struck when racial tensions between these poor immigrants and the city's white population came to a head.

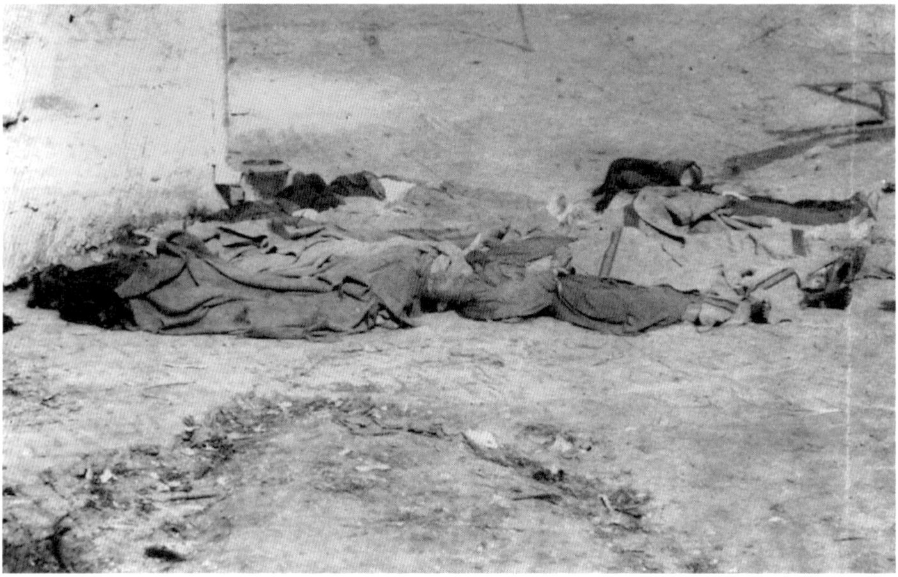

One of the darkest chapters in Los Angeles history came on October 24, 1871. Following a skirmish between two rival Chinese *tongs* that resulted in the death of a white rancher, nineteen Chinese men and boys were brutally massacred. Here some of the bodies can be seen covered in cloth in the immediate aftermath of the event. *Courtesy the Los Angeles Public Library.*

On October 24, 1871, rival Chinese gangs (or *tongs*) got into a heated argument that required the intervention of Los Angeles's constables. During the fray, a white rancher by the name of Robert Thompson was killed; it is still debated whether he was shot intentionally or accidentally. Almost immediately, a mob of five hundred stormed Calle de los Negros. Chinese immigrants were indiscriminately taken captive, dragged through the streets or hanged. Homes and stores were broken into and their goods and money looted. When the night was over, nineteen Chinese were dead.

With the exception of one man, no one killed was involved in the initial fight that left Robert Thompson dead; in fact, those involved in his murder fled the scene as soon as it happened. Bodies were mutilated after death, with fingers being cut off to remove valuable rings. Some of the victims were children. Although some white men, including Sheriff James Burns and the future founder of the University of Southern California (USC), Robert Widney, attempted to stop the massacre, they were quickly overwhelmed by the racially charged mob.

Only eight white men were ever convicted in the massacre, and their sentences were overturned on a technicality; they spent less than two years in San Quentin for their crimes. Today, the largest mass lynching in American history remains an obscure footnote in Los Angeles's history, with many residents unaware of the heinous crimes that once took place in the heart of the city.

POINT FERMIN LIGHTHOUSE

Point Fermin Lighthouse is located on a bluff overlooking San Pedro Bay. Constructed in 1874 (although the original plans for a lighthouse on the site date back to 1854), the Point Fermin Lighthouse was designed in the Stick style of Victorian architecture, which predated the more famous Queen Anne style.

The architect of Point Fermin Lighthouse, Paul J. Pelz (best known for the Thomas Jefferson Building of the Library of Congress), also designed five sister lighthouses with nearly identical designs: East Brother Island Lighthouse in Richmond, California; Point Adams Lighthouse in southern Washington State; Hereford Inlet Lighthouse in North Wildwood, New Jersey; Point Hueneme Lighthouse near Santa Barbara, California; and Mare Island Lighthouse, near San Francisco, California.

Point Fermin Lighthouse was closed during World War II for fear of an invasion from Japan; following the war, the lighthouse fell into disrepair and was threatened with demolition. In 1974, just in time for its 100th anniversary, the lighthouse was fully refurbished to its original appearance.

Although not frequently associated with the West Coast, lighthouses played a significant role in shaping Los Angeles's harbor. Angels Gate Lighthouse, located on the San Pedro breakwater, wouldn't be constructed until 1913; for much of San Pedro's early history, then, Point Fermin Lighthouse was the only navigational aid that sailors had. Today, by offering free tours of the building, the Point Fermin Lighthouse Society helps to preserve this incredibly historic building for all to enjoy.

EASTLAKE AND WESTLAKE PARKS

To a current resident of Los Angeles, the names Eastlake Park and Westlake Park might seem unfamiliar, as neither retains its original name from the Victorian era. However, both are still prominent local landmarks more than a century after they were founded.

Eastlake Park, now known as Lincoln Park, was originally land owned by John Strother Griffin, a surgeon who was on General Stephen Watts Kearney's expedition from New Mexico to California. The property was originally designated as a rail yard for the Southern Pacific Railroad; because of the marshy quality of the land, this plan was deemed infeasible. After almost a decade of public pressure to turn the site into a public park, a three-year landscaping project was begun in 1889. Its centerpiece was a manmade lake located in the center of the park.

Eastlake Park was soon called a "garden-like resort" by the *Los Angeles Times*, and within a few years, there was a bandstand, a boathouse and other amenities for visitors. It was considered by some to be the finest park in all of Los Angeles for the first few decades of the twentieth century and even led to the development of a zoo and small amusement park on the site. In 1917, the name of the park was changed to Lincoln Park after nearby Lincoln High School.

On the other side of downtown Los Angeles is MacArthur Park, originally known as Westlake Park. Originally swampland that was for many years used as a garbage dump, a four-year restorative project on the site was begun in 1886 with the intention of turning Westlake into an attraction. The plan

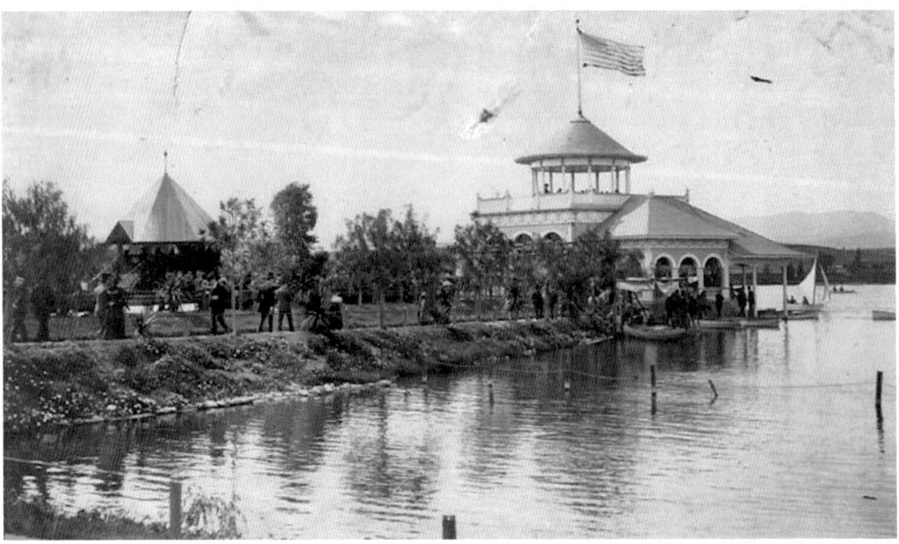

From its inception in the 1880s until 1942, MacArthur Park was known as Westlake Park. Originally swampland, the park was quickly turned into something of a resort destination (as seen in this 1896 photo). The area surrounding Westlake Park was once referred to as the "Champs-Élysées of Los Angeles." *Courtesy the Los Angeles Public Library.*

worked, and when it opened on Thanksgiving Day in 1890, Westlake Park (so named because of its location on the western outskirts of the city) was immediately hailed as one of the finest in the city.

By the middle of the 1890s, both a boathouse and a bandstand had been built in the park; the neighborhood around the park (fittingly called Westlake to this day) became known as the "Champs-Élysées of Los Angeles." Prominent locals, including *Los Angeles Times* editor Harrison Gray Otis, were among the area's residents around the turn of the twentieth century.

In 1934, the park was divided by Wilshire Boulevard, which had originally ended on the west side of Westlake Park. In 1942, the park's name was changed to honor General Douglas MacArthur in the midst of World War II. Since then, the park has developed a dangerous reputation due to its association with gang culture; however, it is important to remember its prominent role in Los Angeles's Victorian past, when it was considered one of the most fashionable locales in the entire city.

A TALE OF TWO UNIVERSITIES

Judge Robert Maclay Widney began searching for suitable land for a university as early as 1871. Widney, who had moved to California in 1868, felt that despite the "Wild West" nature of Los Angeles, there was still hope for an institute of higher education to be established in the city, especially after the success of St. Vincent's.

Initially, Southern California pioneer Abel Stearns was interested in donating land for such a place. However, his death in 1871 forced Widney to look to other sources. The Panic of 1873, which slowed economic development throughout the city, quickly halted any hope of establishing his university. Once the depression had subsided by 1879, Judge Widney again began to map out plans. In May 1879, Widney met with three men—Dr. Joseph P. Widney (the brother of Judge Robert Widney), E.F. Spence and A.M. Hough—to decide on questions such as where the university should be located and where to find funding.

A total of 308 acres of land for the university was donated by three prominent Los Angeles citizens: Ozro W. Childs, John G. Downey and Isaias W. Hellman. These three men came from different religious backgrounds (Protestant, Catholic and Jewish, respectively), but all felt strongly about the need for an institution of higher learning in

Los Angeles. Childs, who was born in Vermont and became a noted horticulturalist later in life, helped to construct the city's irrigation ditches and received a large parcel of land in return. Downey, an Irishman, helped found the Los Angeles Water Company and briefly served as the governor of California. Hellman, a Bavarian-born banker, helped establish Los Angeles's first synagogue before his involvement with USC.

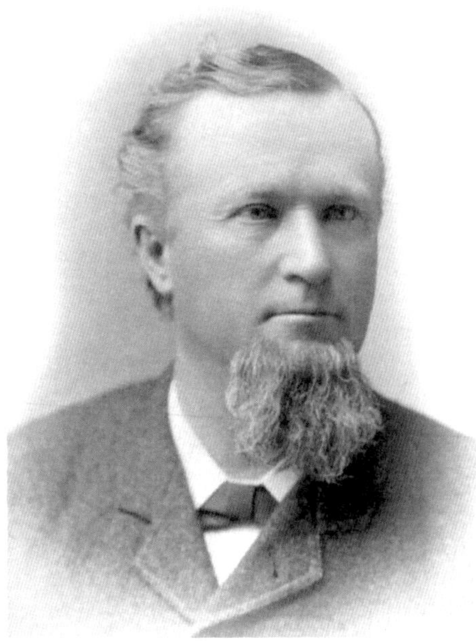

Judge Robert Maclay Widney was a prominent Los Angeles resident whose accomplishments included the founding of the University of Southern California. An eight-and-a-half-foot-tall statue of Widney was placed on USC's campus in 2014. *Courtesy the University of California–Berkeley.*

On July 29, 1879, the official trust deed for the University of Southern California was drawn up by Childs, Downey and Hellman. The first trustees of the university consisted of the four men who had met in May, along with G.B. Compton and Marion McKinley Bovard, who would go on to be the university's first president.

When the university first opened its doors to students in 1880, it consisted of only one structure. The original university building was a two-story, wooden Italianate structure constructed on the original plot of land given to the university. Designed by architects Ezra F. Kysor and Octavius Morgan at a cost of only $5,060, the cornerstone was laid on September 4, 1880. Almost one-tenth of the population of Los Angeles attended the ceremony to see the partially completed building, which was finished on October 4 (classes began two days later). The school started with only fifty-three students, and all classes were held in this one building.

Over the years, the original university building has served a number of purposes and has been moved three times around campus. In 1977, the Widney Alumni Hall (as it is now called) underwent a complete renovation, which included the removal of the 1890s additions, thus restoring the building to its original appearance.

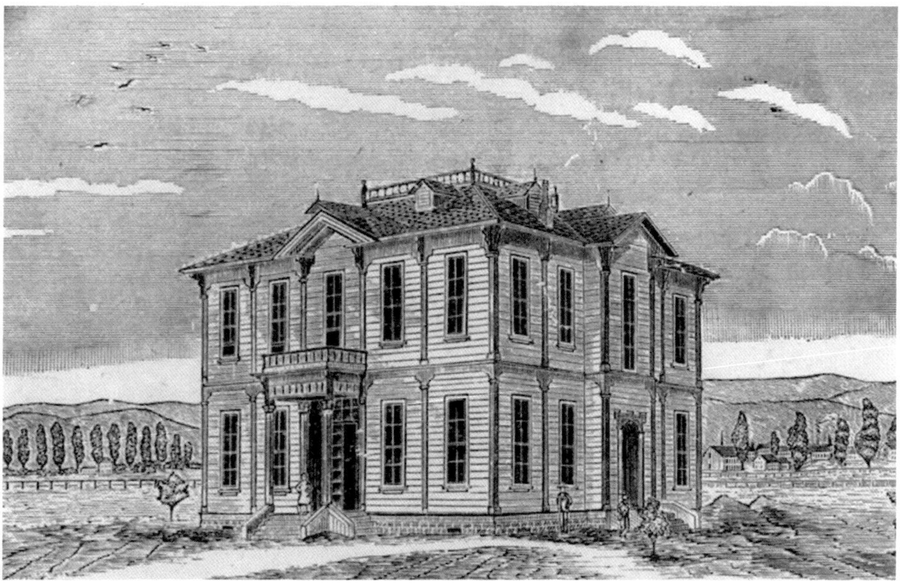

USC's first building was constructed in 1880 at a cost of only $5,060. Today, this building is known as Widney Alumni Hall and is the oldest collegiate building still standing in Southern California. *Courtesy the Los Angeles Public Library.*

Although several other wooden structures were built in the years after USC was founded, the school's first brick building—for which the campus is famous—was built in 1884, the same year that USC graduated its first three students. The USC College of Medicine would be founded the following year; today it is one of the premier medical programs in Southern California.

Since its humble founding in 1880, USC has continued to grow and develop into one of the top universities in the state of California, and the campus has changed drastically. But the fact that the school's first building—which is also the oldest university building in Southern California—is still standing firmly roots USC's heritage in the Victorian era.

USC wasn't the only school to have been founded during the 1880s; during the following year, crosstown rival UCLA got its start as well, although in a very different form. Several decades prior, in 1862, the California State Normal School got its start as a teaching college in San Francisco. By 1881, at the urging of the city's residents, Los Angeles was granted a southern branch of the school.

The following August, the Los Angeles branch opened and dedicated its new campus, located on the present site of the main branch of the public

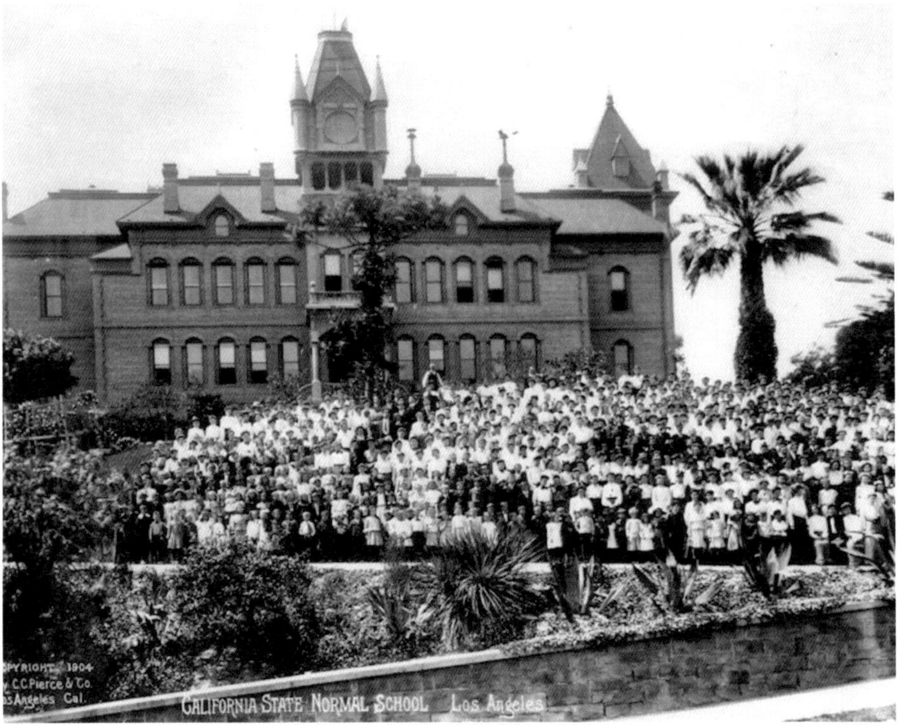

UCLA's predecessor, the California State Normal School, is seen here with a large gathering of teachers and students in front of it. The structure was demolished to make way for the new Los Angeles Public Library, which opened in 1926. *Courtesy the Los Angeles Public Library.*

library (Fifth Street and Grand Avenue). The original building, as well as several additions made soon after, was designed in a Collegiate Gothic style reminiscent of the nearby St. Vincent's. Because it was located on what was called "Normal Hill," adjacent to Bunker Hill, the school's already impressive architecture was greatly enhanced.

At the Normal School's peak, it was one of Southern California's most prominent institutions of higher education. Tuition was free, provided attendees covered their own room and board. There was even an elementary school attached so that teachers in training could practice their trade without having to leave the campus.

In the first decades of the twentieth century, the city began to spring up around what had once been a fairly remote campus. The need for more land soon became apparent, and in 1914, the Normal School moved to a new site at Vermont Avenue between Melrose Avenue and Santa Monica Boulevard. In 1919, the school merged with the University of California, and ten years later, the new University of California–Los Angeles moved to its present location in Westwood.

The former Normal School campus is now Los Angeles City College, although Normal Avenue still gives a hint to the campus's former occupant. As for Normal Hill, it was leveled soon after the Normal School moved, and several years later, a new architectural landmark—the Los Angeles Public Library—took its former spot.

ST. VIBIANA'S

The Cathedral of St. Vibiana, which is located at 214 South Main Street, was the city's first Catholic Church constructed after *La Iglesia de Nuestra Señora la Reina de los Ángeles*, more commonly known as the Plaza Church. W.J. Mathews and E.F. Kysor, Los Angeles's first prominent architect, designed the building in a combination of Baroque and Italianate styles—a sharp contrast to the region's Spanish Catholic missions. Constructed at an incredible sum of $80,000 in 1876 (approximately $1.7 million in 2014), the Cathedral St. Vibiana held 10 percent of Los Angeles's population at the time and immediately became one of the city's landmark buildings.

St. Vibiana is not a saint many people have heard of, so the naming of such a prominent cathedral after her may seem strange. Vibiana's remains were discovered in a Roman catacomb in 1851; writing on her third-century tomb simply read, "to the soul of the innocent and pure Vibiana" alongside a laurel wreath (a symbol of martyrdom). Pope Pius IX quickly declared her a saint, despite the fact that almost nothing was known about her life. Because of this fact, Vibiana is sometimes referred to as the "Patron Saint of Nobodies"—with no backstory, there is a universality to her life to which many can relate.

During the nineteenth century, cathedrals considered it almost a necessity to hold a saint's relics as a testament to their holiness. An archdiocese as large as Monterey–Los Angeles quickly realized the opportunity presented by the discovery of a new saint and quickly got in touch with the Vatican. Vibiana's relics were sent to California shortly thereafter, and once the Cathedral of St. Vibiana opened in 1876, her remains were placed in a sarcophagus above the church's altar.

Mathews and Kysor's stunningly designed cathedral served Los Angeles's Catholics until the 1990s, when the 1994 Northridge Earthquake

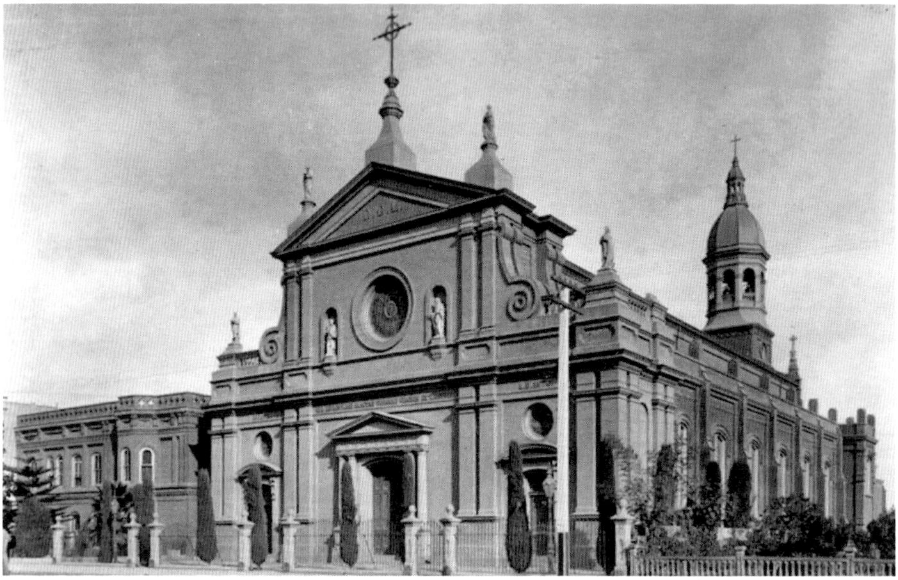

Known for its ornate Baroque and Italianate architecture, St. Vibiana's was Los Angeles's first cathedral. In the mid-1990s, the building was transferred to the city of Los Angeles by the Catholic Church in exchange for land to build a new cathedral. *Courtesy the Los Angeles Public Library.*

severely damaged the building. The archdiocese began looking into constructing a new cathedral on the same site, but preservationists quickly stepped in to prevent the old structure from being torn down. Eventually, a compromise was reached that allowed the Catholic Church to build a new cathedral elsewhere in downtown, while St. Vibiana's was converted to a public event space.

The former cathedral's renovation was completed in 2005, while the original cupola was returned to the bell tower two years later. Today, Vibiana's is one of the most remarkable Victorian structures left in the city and is one of downtown's only buildings to have survived more than a century of development and modernization. Alongside the nearby Pico House and Bradbury Building, it is, in the opinion of the author, one of the three most significant Victorian buildings left in the heart of the city.

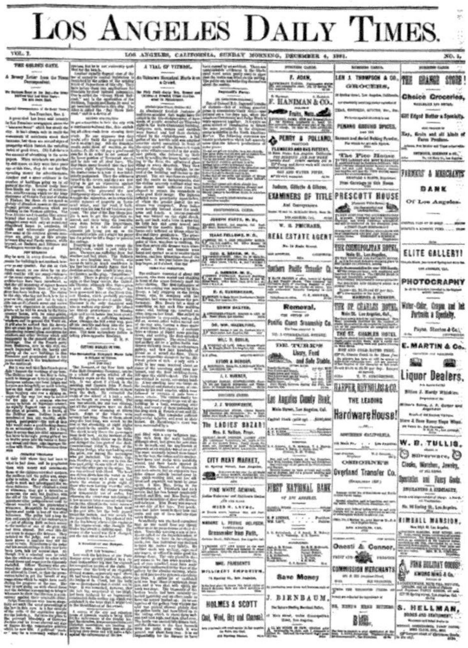

LOS ANGELES DAILY TIMES.

VOL. I. LOS ANGELES, CALIFORNIA, SUNDAY MORNING, DECEMBER 4, 1881. NO. 1.

The front page of the first edition of the *Los Angeles Times* on December 4, 1881. Under the leadership of newspaper mogul Harrison Gray Otis, the *Times* quickly became successful and remains the city's only major daily paper. *Courtesy the* Los Angeles Times.

THE *LOS ANGELES DAILY TIMES*

Today, the *Los Angeles Times* is the city's sole major daily paper. For much of Los Angeles's history, there were a number of competing papers. It was thirty years after Los Angeles's first newspaper was started that two men, Nathan Cole Jr. and Thomas Gardiner, founded the *Los Angeles Daily Times*. Their first issue was published on December 4, 1881; however, the paper quickly ran into financial troubles, and Cole and Gardiner were forced to relinquish ownership.

The following year, Harrison Gray Otis, a former Union captain during the Civil War, moved his family from Santa Barbara to Los Angeles to take over the paper's operations. Otis also became the managing editor of the *Weekly Mirror*, with which the *Times* would later merge into the Times-Mirror Company. Otis would continue to successfully run the *Los Angeles Times*, often with a strong Republican bias, until his death in 1917, at which point the paper was taken over by his son-in-law, Harry Chandler. The Chandler era would continue with Harry's son, Norman, for much of the twentieth century, although today the dynastic era of Los Angeles's newspapers is a thing of the past.

ROSEDALE CEMETERY

In 1884, at the very end of the period covered in this chapter, a sixty-five-acre cemetery was opened between Venice and Washington Boulevards, Normandie Avenue and Catalina Street. Although Los Angeles already had a number of cemeteries, Rosedale Cemetery was unique in several ways.

First, Rosedale Cemetery was the first in the city that did not exclude interments based on religion or race, a progressive notion for the 1880s. It was also the city's first so-called lawn cemetery. Although commonplace today, during the nineteenth century many cemeteries were still constructed in the midst of urban settings, and the concept of using open space and landscaping for cemeteries was still considered somewhat novel.

Today, Angelus-Rosedale Cemetery (as it has been known since 1993) is the final resting place of many prominent pioneers, politicians, entertainers and other civic and social leaders. Six former mayors are buried at the cemetery, as is Phineas Banning (discussed extensively in the previous chapter), Robert Widney (the founder of the University of Southern California) and David Burbank (the father of Burbank).

Isaac Newton Van Nuys

What Phineas Banning was to the Port of Los Angeles, Isaac Newton Van Nuys was to the San Fernando Valley. Born on November 20, 1836, in West Sparta, New York, Van Nuys was the first member of his family to immigrate to California when he made the move in 1865. When he moved to Los Angeles in 1871, he promptly bought into the San Fernando Valley Farm Home Stead Association—a collective headed by Isaac Lankershim that owned sixty thousand acres in the San Fernando Valley.

Van Nuys moved to the Valley in 1873 and quickly began implementing dryland farming on the property. Within several years, his business ventures were already beginning to pay off. By 1876, he had sent the first-ever shipment of wheat from the Port of Los Angeles, which incidentally was also the first American grain ever sent to Europe.

Isaac Newton Van Nuys along with Lankershim's son, James Boon Lankershim, continued to grow their empire. The year 1880 saw the founding of the Los Angeles Farming and Milling Company, a successor to the Home Stead Association into which Van Nuys had bought only nine years earlier. Van Nuys quickly rose in prominence in the community, and within a short while, he had become not only a business leader but also a civic leader. It was also in 1880 that Van Nuys married Susanna Lankershim, the daughter of Isaac Lankershim and sister of James Boon Lankershim.

As the twentieth century began, land speculation in the San Fernando Valley began to rise steadily, particularly after plans for the Los Angeles

Aqueduct promised civic growth in the valley. During the last years of his life, Van Nuys was influential in the acquisition of large tracts of land by the Los Angeles Suburban Homes Company. Van Nuys, the city named in his honor, was founded in 1911—only two years before his death at the age of seventy-five.

Van Nuys's shrewd business practices and ceaseless dedication to the San Fernando Valley ensured that the region would become a success, as evidenced by the 1.8 million people living there today. Without his involvement in the area's development, the course of the San Fernando Valley's history would undoubtedly have been very different.

For the first time in its history, Los Angeles during the 1870s grew to resemble an American city. Although still not beyond having unspeakable atrocities such as the Chinese Massacre, there was a concerted effort by prominent locals for the rise of institutions that were religious and educational in nature (some of which, such as USC, the *Los Angeles Times* and the Archdiocese of Los Angeles, are still around today). On an aesthetic note, this period also saw the first influence of architecture from the East Coast, with buildings such as the Pico House being designed in an Italianate style that showed an emulation of established American cities—further evidence of the major strides Los Angeles was taking toward becoming a cultural center.

CHAPTER 4

HEIGHT OF THE VICTORIAN ERA, 1885–1901

VICTORIAN STEREOTYPES

Los Angeles during the last decade and a half of the twentieth century is the closest the city ever came to resembling a stereotypically "Victorian" city. Queen Anne architecture—a style closely associated with the era—spread in both commercial and residential situations. New technology, very often correlated with the Victorian era, also flourished in Los Angeles; streetcars,

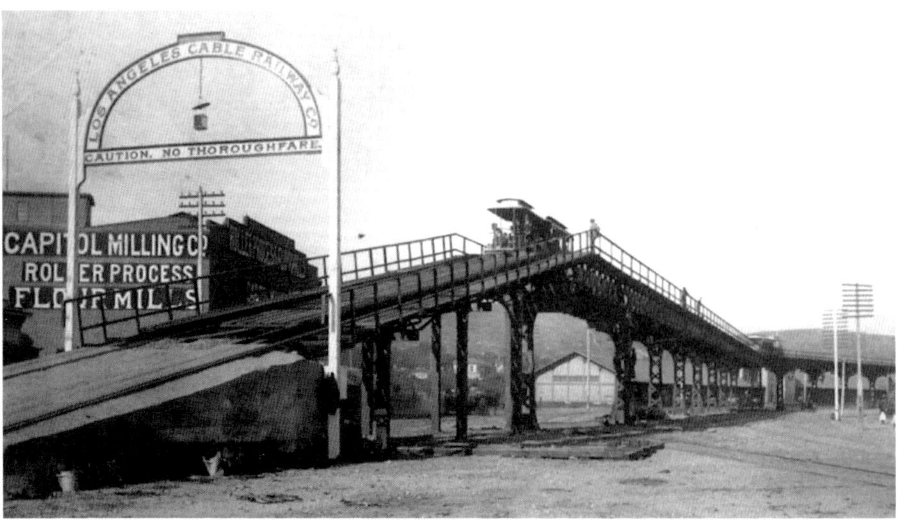

incline railways, amusement parks and other features that had been impossibilities just a few years earlier soon sprung up around the county. The East Coast influence that had begun to show itself during the 1870s and early 1880s developed into a full-blown emulation of established cities.

A NEW CIVIC CENTER

During the 1880s, as population rose steadily, Los Angeles began to develop a civic center fitting for a city of its size. Prior to this time, many governmental functions were held in makeshift quarters. It was not until relatively late in the Victorian period that large-scale dedicated public buildings began to be constructed.

Throughout the city's history, Los Angeles's city hall moved a number of times, from humble beginnings in rented hotel rooms to the current Art Deco landmark skyscraper. Largely forgotten, however, was the current city hall's predecessor—one of a number of large-scale public buildings built during the Victorian era.

As the city rapidly grew in the 1880s, the need for a larger city hall became more apparent. After a short stint in a building located where the *Los Angeles Times* building is today, plans were drawn up for a larger structure at 226 South Broadway. Eugene Caukin and Solomon Haas, an architectural duo that specialized in Richardsonian Romanesque architecture, were tasked with coming up with a design.

The $150,000 structure, completed and opened in 1888, immediately became one of the dominant features of the Los Angeles skyline. The Romanesque building, composed of brick and red sandstone, was by all accounts an impressive and imposing sight. In the days before high-rises dominated downtown, the building's street-front tower could be seen from miles around, and the style of architecture set a precedent for other public buildings to come several years later.

By the time the 1920s rolled around, Romanesque architecture was looked on as outdated, and just as was the case in the 1880s, the city needed more modern facilities for its civic government. In 1927, John and Donald

Opposite: One of Los Angeles's early cable cars is seen here at the foot of the Spring Street Bridge. During the 1880s and 1890s, the city had several lines such as this that connected downtown to the rapidly developing suburbs. *Courtesy the Los Angeles Public Library.*

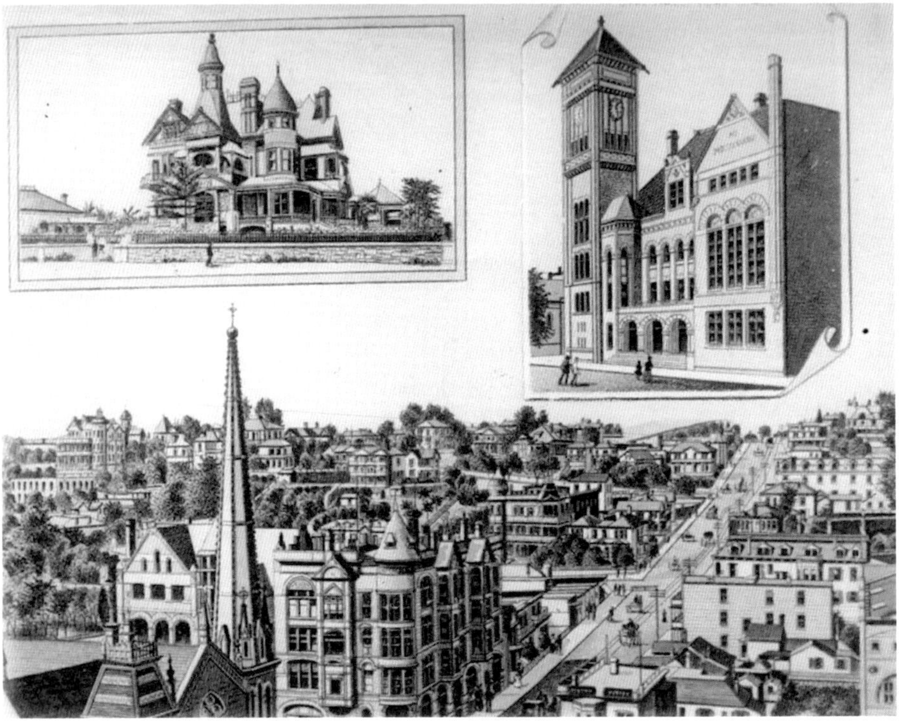

This drawing shows some of Los Angeles's prominent landmarks in the late 1880s, including a Victorian mansion (thought to be the Hale House) and the 1888 city hall. Below these two buildings is an aerial view of the fledgling city. *Courtesy the Los Angeles Public Library.*

Parkinson designed the current Art Deco structure several blocks away, and when it was completed the following year, an auction was held to dispose of the old building's fixtures and furniture. Within several months, demolition had begun, and the building that had served as the heart of the city for four decades quickly became a footnote in history books.

Jonathan Temple, one of the most prominent figures in early Los Angeles history, was responsible for building the city's first courthouse. Designed as a market and Los Angeles's first theater, the building (which stood between 1859 and 1891) was soon rented out by the government for use as a courthouse. Temple's courthouse was affectionately known as the "Clock Tower Courthouse" because of its unique architecture and quickly became a local landmark. However, as the city rapidly grew, the need for a new courthouse was quickly realized by local residents.

The new structure, a major addition to the fledgling city, was designed by the prominent firm of Curlett, Eisen and Cuthbertson. It was located

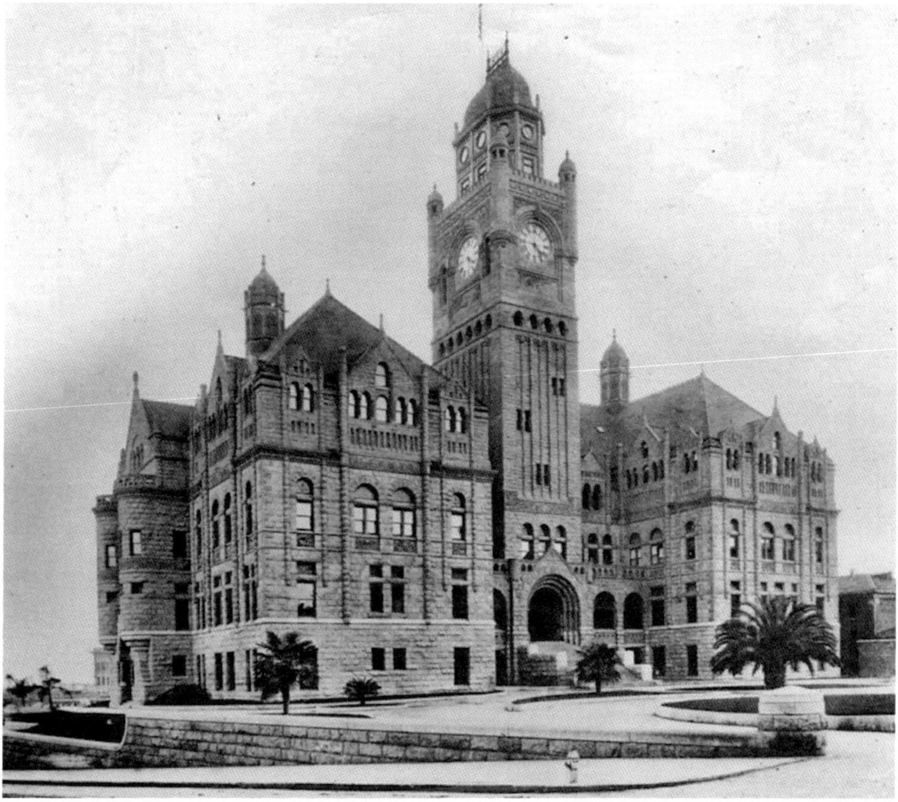

Designed in a similar architectural style as the nearby city hall, Los Angeles's 1891 courthouse was also part of the large building boom at the end of the nineteenth century. Irreparable damage in the 1933 Long Beach Earthquake forced its demolition. *Courtesy the Los Angeles Public Library.*

on Poundcake Hill (southeast corner of Temple Street and Broadway); the high school building was moved to make way for the new courthouse. Matching the Richardsonian Romanesque architecture of the nearby city hall, the courthouse featured striking sandstone walls, turreted entrances and a central clock tower.

The sandstone courthouse was one of the most architecturally impressive buildings in the city's history, but as fate would have it, the building was irreparably damaged in the 1933 Long Beach Earthquake. After standing vacant for several years, the Works Progress Administration was tasked with its demolition. Fortunately, although the building was lost, the clock face was saved and placed on display in the Natural History Museum of Los Angeles County, preserving a small piece of the building's legacy. For more than

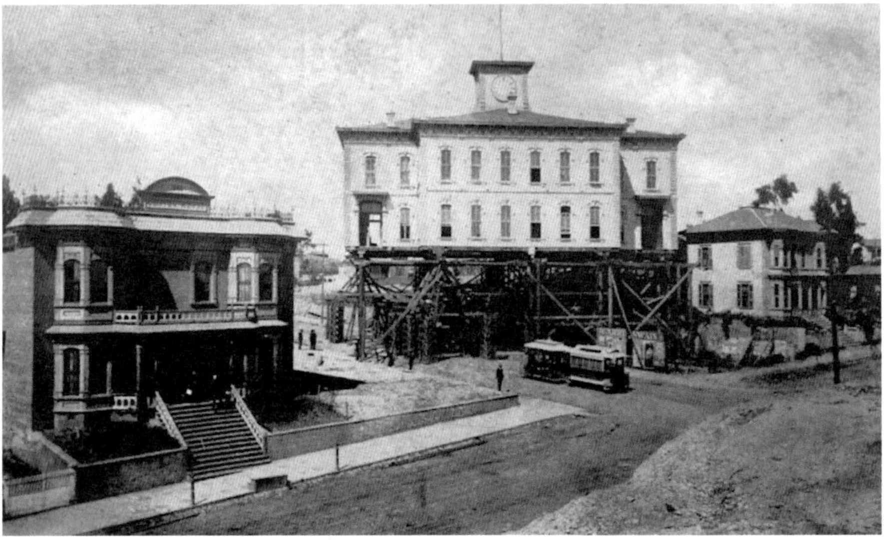

The original Los Angeles High School, built in 1873, is seen here in transit from Poundcake Hill to nearby Fort Moore Hill. Funding to move the school ran out midway through the process, so the school was placed on risers to allow streetcars to run underneath it (seen here). *Courtesy the Los Angeles Public Library.*

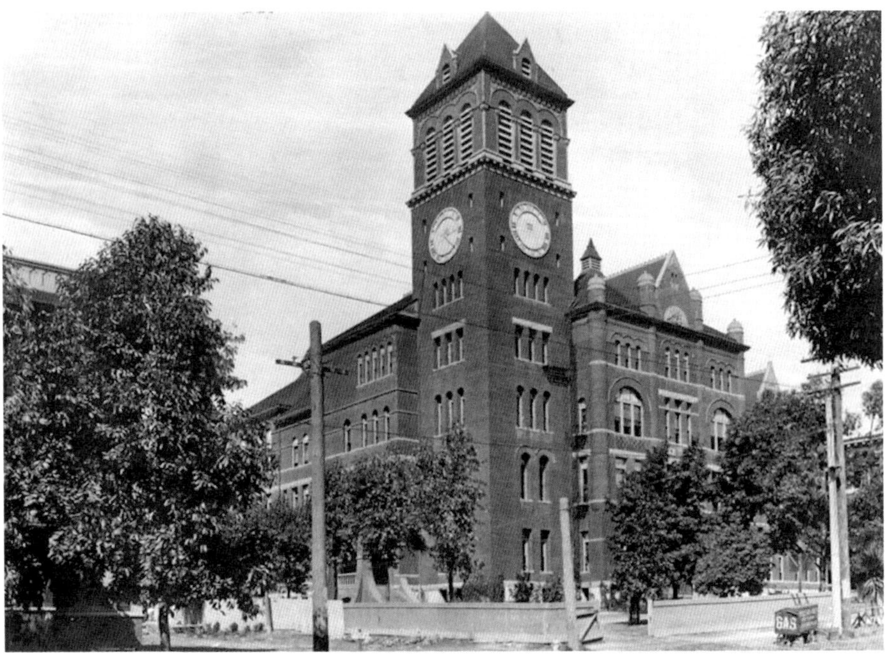

Los Angeles's 1891 high school was designed in a Romanesque style similar to other governmental buildings of the time. Located atop Fort Moore Hill, the imposing brick building was demolished in the late 1940s to make way for the 101 Freeway. *Courtesy the Los Angeles Public Library.*

two decades, Los Angeles functioned without a county courthouse, until a new structure was opened at the beginning of 1959 (now the Stanley Mosk County Courthouse).

As mentioned earlier, Los Angeles's first high school had to be moved from its location on Poundcake Hill in 1886 in order to make way for the new courthouse. The school was constructed at this location beginning in 1872; the $19,000 structure opened the following year and graduated its first class of seven students in 1875. Because of its location atop the hill, students had to climb a long flight of stairs in order to reach the school.

When it was deemed necessary to move the high school, a contractor by the name of Mr. Hickam was hired to move the building to a nearby location. Using a system of horse-drawn rollers, Hickam was only able to move the school as far as Temple Street before running out of money. Because of the inconvenience of having a schoolhouse in the middle of the street, risers were used to allow the streetcars to run underneath the building. As absurd as it sounds, the school remained like this for some time before being moved out of the road.

Eventually, by 1891, a new high school had been opened on top of Fort Moore Hill. Built from red brick and sporting a large clock tower, it was visually cohesive with the city's other large buildings from this time. Because of its prominent location, this building is visible in many photos taken of the city from the 1890s on.

Between the time of the Mexican-American War and the construction of the high school, Fort Moore Hill was used as the city's first Protestant graveyard; when the school was built, the city neglected to remove the remains and headstones for several years, and students would sometimes eat their lunch sitting among the graves.

As the city began to sprawl in the early twentieth century, Los Angeles High School moved to its current Olympic Boulevard location in 1917. The 1891 building became a high school for troubled students before finally being demolished in the late 1940s to make way for the 101 Freeway. At the time, it was the last of Los Angeles's great Victorian public buildings to be standing.

THE BRADBURY BUILDING

One of the most celebrated buildings in Los Angeles—from a historic and architectural standpoint—is the Bradbury Building, located on the southeast corner of Broadway and Third Street. In a city that retained few

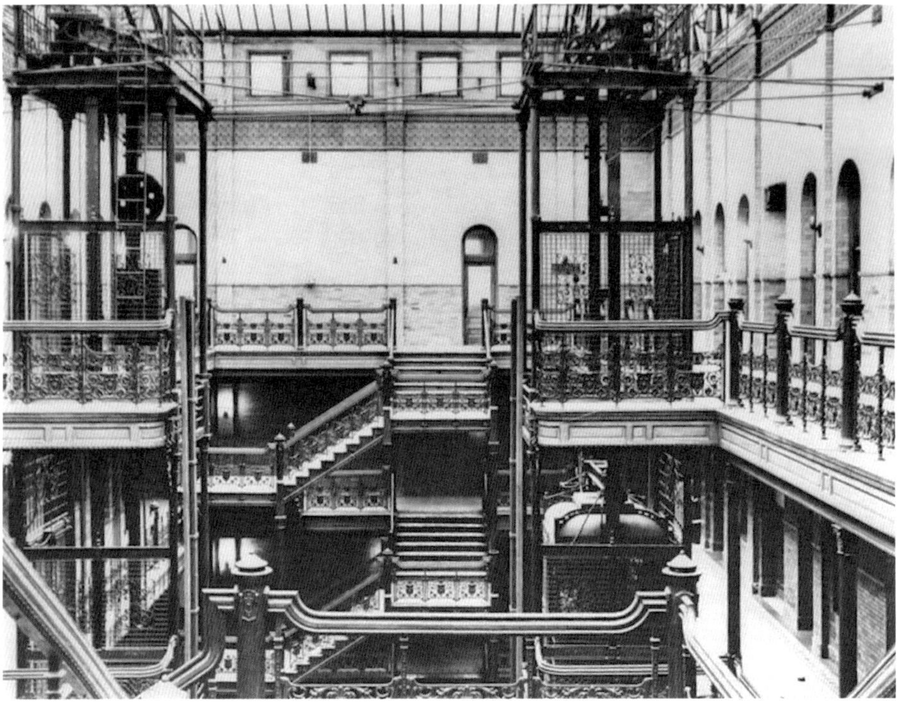

The interior of the Bradbury Building features wrought iron that was crafted in France and exhibited at the 1893 World's Fair before its installation in Los Angeles. The building's glass ceiling allows natural light to illuminate the lobby. *Courtesy the Los Angeles Public Library.*

of its Victorian landmarks (particularly commercial buildings), the Bradbury Building stands out as a true historic gem.

From the outside, the Bradbury Building does not appear particularly spectacular. The building is unique in that its construction was subtly inspired by Richardsonian Romanesque architecture, a style that was never overwhelmingly popular on the West Coast. However, it is the inside of the Bradbury Building that is so remarkable, with one author calling it "one of the most beautiful interior spaces to be found in Los Angeles."

The idea for such an opulent building came from gold magnate Lewis L. Bradbury, for whom the building is named. Originally, one of Los Angeles's most prominent architects, Sumner P. Hunt, was hired for the job. Bradbury was unhappy with Hunt's finished plans, so he hired one of Hunt's draftsmen, George H. Wyman, to redesign the structure.

Whether Wyman actually changed Hunt's design is a matter of debate to this day, and the fact that Wyman was largely unsuccessful as an

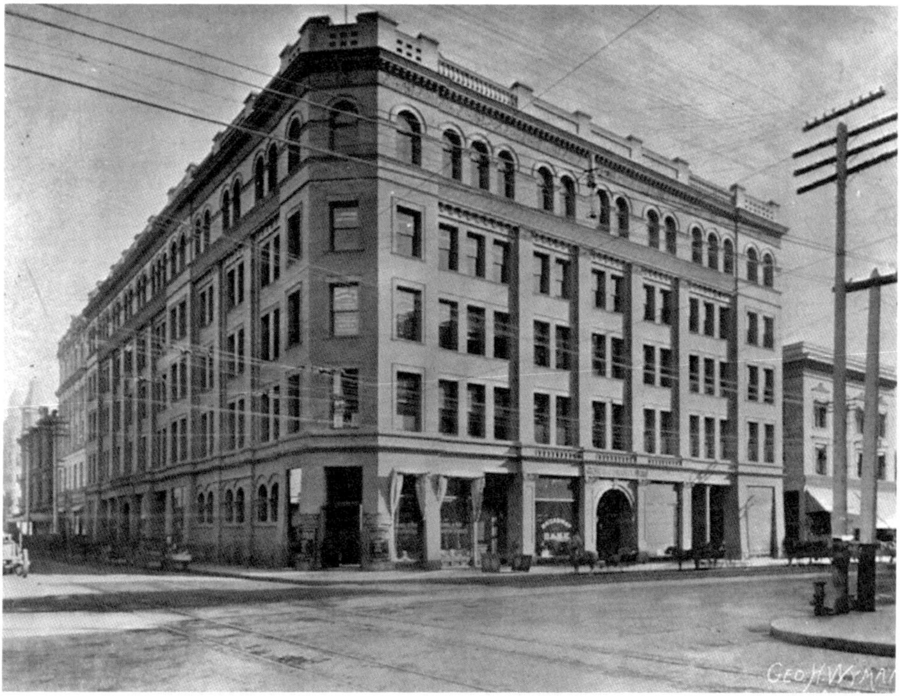

Perhaps Los Angeles's most celebrated Victorian landmark, the Bradbury Building's modest exterior is sharply contrasted by its ornate interior design. The building has been used in countless movies and television because it still manages to evoke the nineteenth century. *Courtesy the Los Angeles Public Library.*

architect later in life suggests that Hunt was primarily responsible for the building's unique design. When offered the job, Wyman initially refused; however, after allegedly receiving a message from his deceased brother via planchette, he reconsidered Bradbury's offer.

Regardless of the circumstances behind the building's design, what is known is that the Bradbury Building opened in 1893, only months after Bradbury's death the previous year. Although the building's original budget was $175,000, the final cost was closer to $500,000 due to unforeseen difficulties and Bradbury's insistence on the best possible materials.

The building's narrow entrances lead into a naturally lit court that still appears almost exactly like it did more than 120 years ago. The building's wrought iron, which appears everywhere from the staircases to the mail chutes, was made in France and exhibited at the 1893 Columbian Exposition in Chicago before being installed. Instead of a traditional roof, the building features a massive skylight that illuminates the entire interior. Decorative tiles and open-air elevators complete the building's dazzling design.

The Bradbury Building has been completely refurbished in recent decades and presently serves as a tourist attraction for many visitors to the downtown area. Countless movies (notably *Chinatown*, *Blade Runner* and *The Artist*), commercials, music videos and television shows have been shot in the building, which is still primarily used as private offices.

CASA DE ROSAS

Located a stone's throw from the University of California, Casa de Rosas (2608 South Hoover Street) has one of the most diverse and varied histories of any building in Los Angeles. Formally known as the Sunshine Mission, it was constructed in 1893 and was the first building ever designed by Sumner P. Hunt, who would go on to become one of the city's most prolific architects. Sunshine Mission is important architecturally because it is one of the earliest examples of Mission Revival architecture; it is also one of the finest surviving examples of the style in Southern California.

The main building was built as the home of the Froebel Institute. Friedrich Froebel, who lived from 1782 to 1852, was a German pedagogue who developed the concept of the kindergarten. This makes Casa De Rosas one of the earliest kindergartens in California; it would take the state another six years to make it a part of public school curriculum. The building nearly burned down in 1903, however, and was reopened in 1904 as the prestigious Girls Collegiate Boarding School.

The building's post-Victorian history is so unique that it is worth mentioning briefly. By the 1930s, Casa de Rosas was functioning as a hotel and restaurant (featuring complete dinners for fifty cents and filet mignon for sixty-five cents); this is also where the international student population of USC lived at the time. It was again repurposed in the early 1940s, when it was used as barracks for soldiers in World War II. After being put up for sale, it was purchased in November 1950 by L. Ron Hubbard as a center for his Dianetic Research Foundation.

The building changed hands for the last time in late 1950, when Sister Essie Binkley West purchased it. West, known as the "Angel of Skid Row," had been helping needy young women and unwed mothers for decades. Despite decades of dilapidation and disrepair, as well as two arson attempts in 1984 and 1987, the building is currently being refurbished to its original appearance, making it a remarkable survival story of one of Los Angeles's most storied Victorian buildings.

GRIFFITH PARK

Los Angeles's largest municipally owned park, and one of the largest such parks in the nation, is Griffith Park. Although a natural oasis today, surrounded completely by urban development, Griffith Park's history is steeped in crime and mystery.

Originally, the land that is currently Griffith Park, as well as parts of Hollywood and Los Feliz, was known as Rancho Los Feliz. Colonel Griffith J. Griffith, who had previously made a fortune through mining in Northern California, purchased 4,071 acres of the rancho in 1882. On the property, he established an ostrich farm and quickly began trying to attract people to move to the new developments he was working on.

The conventional story is that the housing burst in the late 1880s caused Colonel Griffith to donate his land to the city; however, there is a much more sinister version of the story that has circulated for more than a century. Allegedly, in 1884, ranch hands working for Griffith claimed to have seen the ghost of Antonio Feliz (the rancho's former owner) riding waves of water down a hillside during a torrential rainstorm.

Following the first apparition, Feliz was also said to be seen on Bee Rock, a prominent geological feature in the eastern part of the park; he was also accused of wreaking havoc with Griffith's herd of ostriches. Deterred by his men's stories, Colonel Griffith supposedly only visited the property during the daytime.

Whatever the reason—whether financial or supernatural—on December 16, 1896, 3,015 acres of Griffith's land was donated to the city as a Christmas present. His only stipulation was that "it must be made a place of rest and relaxation for the masses, a resort for the rank and file, for the plain people."

Griffith's legacy was greatly marred by the 1903 shooting of his wife, Christina, in a Santa Monica hotel. Eventually released from prison, Griffith endeavored to fund a public theater and science hall in the park that bore his name. Not surprisingly, the city refused his gift because of his criminal reputation, and it was not until years after his death that such structures would be constructed (the Greek Theater in 1930 and the Griffith Observatory in 1935).

Although many features of the park are relatively modern developments, the seeds for California's second-largest urban park trace their roots back to Colonel Griffith's initial gift in 1896, at the height of the Victorian era in Los Angeles.

BOYLE HOTEL

Also known as the Cummings Block, the Boyle Hotel (101 North Boyle Avenue) is an important landmark in the history of suburban growth in Los Angeles. Boyle Heights, located across the Los Angeles River from downtown, is one of the city's oldest neighborhoods and benefited immensely from the rise of public transportation during the late twentieth century.

When it was constructed in 1889, the Boyle Hotel quickly became a center of activity in the burgeoning neighborhood. George Cummings, the building's owner, intended for his hotel to cater to the social elite of East Los Angeles during this time. In keeping with the era, architect W.R. Norton designed the building in a unique mixture of Romanesque and Queen Anne styles.

Over the years, the Boyle Hotel fell into a state of disrepair and even lost the top of its hallmark corner turret. In 2007, the site was both declared a Los Angeles Historic-Cultural Monument and purchased by the East Los Angeles Community Corporation, which promptly began a $24.6 million refurbishment of the hotel.

During the five-year project, the architectural integrity of the Cummings Block was restored in full, and in 2012, it was reopened as a mixed-use space featuring housing, commercial space and a cultural center. Today, the Boyle Hotel stands not only as a success story of local preservation but also as, arguably, the finest example of Victorian commercial architecture in Los Angeles east of the river.

EDWARD DOHENY AND THE "DISCOVERY" OF OIL

Few men can claim a larger impact on the history of Los Angeles than Edward Laurence Doheny, who almost single-handedly ushered in an entirely new era when he began drilling for oil. Born on August 10, 1856, in Fond du Lac, Wisconsin, Doheny spent much of his early life prospecting and mining throughout the western United States.

It was during one of these mining stints in Kingston, Arizona, that Doheny met Charles A. Canfield, who would go on to be his longtime business partner. However, by the end of 1891, both men had ended up in Los Angeles deeply in debt. Canfield had lost his small fortune in bad real estate investments, while Doheny was unable to have any success in his mining endeavors.

The rest of Doheny's story is undoubtedly apocryphal, having been told countless times since the events described occurred. Despite its factual accuracy, it has entered the cultural fabric of Los Angeles and deserves to be told here.

Edward Doheny claimed that one day in the fall of 1892, he was living in a hotel downtown—so poor he was unable to pay his rent—when he saw a wagon carrying tar. Doheny stopped the driver to inquire where the tar had come from and what its purpose was. The driver explained that it had come from the Westlake neighborhood and was being used as fuel for a local ice plant. In his own words, Doheny later recounted, "I had found gold and I had found silver and I had found lead, but this ugly-looking substance I felt was the key to something more valuable than any one of these metals."

Doheny and Canfield were too poor to afford land near Westlake, but they purchased a plot near the intersection of West State and Patton Streets (present-day Glendale Boulevard and Colton Street). Unable to purchase proper equipment, Doheny dug the well with a shovel, while Canfield used a pulley system to clear debris from the shaft. After thirty-eight days and digging down 155 feet, the two men finally struck oil. Once the well was completed the following year, it produced forty barrels per day.

Although he is often credited with "discovering" oil in Los Angeles, Doheny's well was by no means the first in the city (oil exploration dates back to at least 1863, when the first unsuccessful attempt at drilling was made). By the time of Doheny's 1892 well, there were about one hundred wells producing oil in Los Angeles County already, although none of them on a particularly large scale.

It should also be mentioned that Doheny was probably not as lucky as he suggested in his story. As someone well acquainted with the geology of the western United States, he would presumably have been aware of the known petroleum reservoirs beneath Los Angeles. It is doubtful that he was simply a random bystander who had a chance encounter with a cart in downtown Los Angeles and suddenly had the idea to begin drilling for oil.

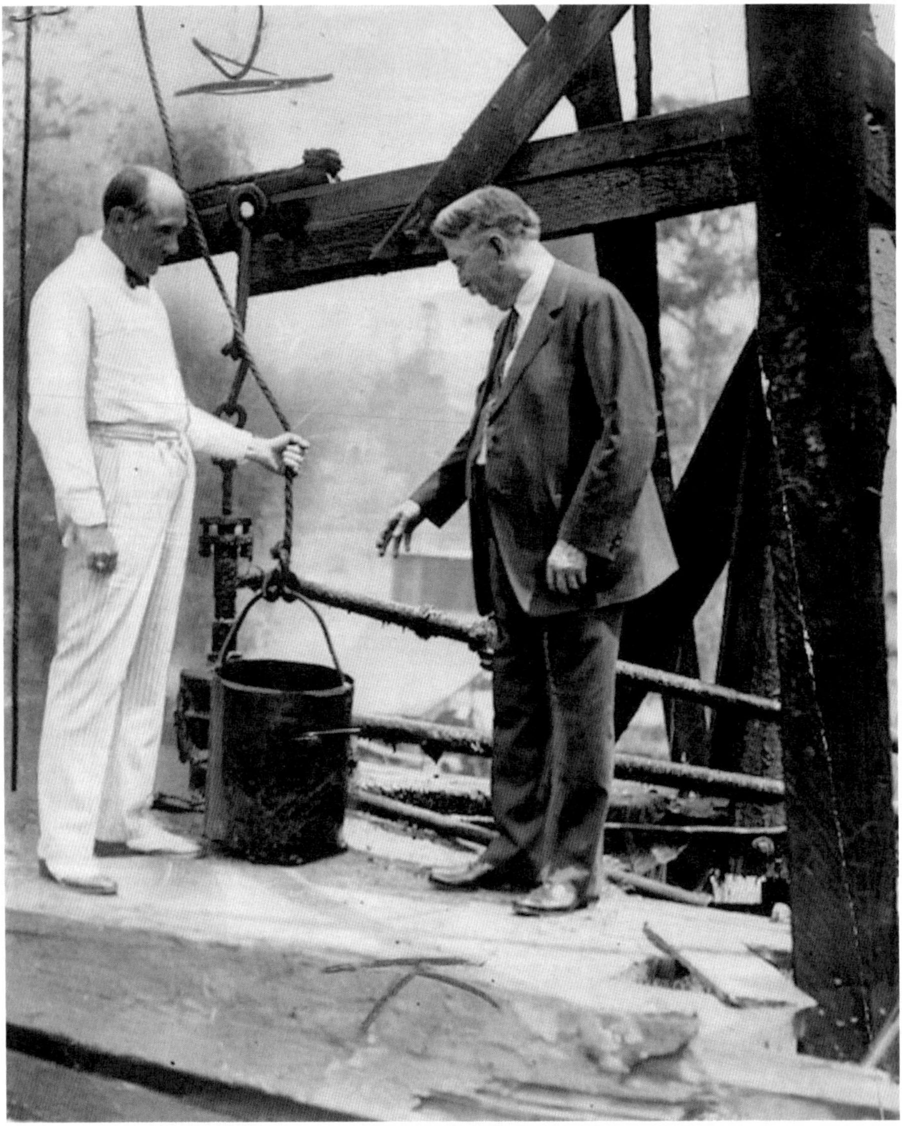

Oil magnate Edward L. Doheny (right) is seen here with his associate Charles Canfield at the site of Los Angeles's first oil well. If not for Doheny's innovation in digging that well in 1892, the history of the city would be markedly different. *Courtesy the Los Angeles Public Library.*

Whatever actually happened in 1892, the details of the story are irrelevant, as Doheny's true legacy came from what he did after the first well began producing oil. By selling oil to local factories, he was able to finance the digging of additional wells in the area—about three hundred within three years.

Although he wasn't the first to find oil in Los Angeles, Doheny was the first to make significant amounts of money from it, and this prompted an oil boom during the early twentieth century that helped put Los Angeles on the map. Much of his later fortune came from wells financed in Mexico that were a direct result of his initial drilling operations in Los Angeles; within a few decades, Doheny went from being broke to being one of the nation's wealthiest men.

By bringing new money, new development and new prominence to the city, the oil boom of the early twentieth century was one of the key factors in the close of the Victorian era of Los Angeles. Although the city had evolved greatly throughout the last decades of the 1800s, it still had major strides to make before becoming a truly modern city; Doheny's utilization of the region's petroleum resources was a major impetus toward the completion of this shift.

Doheny's later years were somewhat tainted by scandal—including the Teapot Dome incident of the early 1920s and the mysterious suicide of his son, Edward Doheny Jr., in 1929 (and the family's subsequent coverup). However, the importance of Doheny on the history of Los Angeles can hardly be overestimated, and it is for his business practices and philanthropy that he can best be remembered.

The period from 1885 to 1901 can be viewed as the height of the Victorian era in Los Angeles, at least in terms of modern stereotypes. At the very least, it was the closest Los Angeles ever came to approaching the grandeur of East Coast cities up until this time. Architecturally and technologically, the influence was apparent in almost every part of the city. Perhaps the crown jewel of this era of Los Angeles's history was the new civic infrastructure that was constructed, consisting of a monumental courthouse, a city hall and a high school—none of which survived past the middle of the twentieth century. However, there are still a fair number of buildings, both downtown and around the city, surviving from this era. They will be covered more in depth later in this book.

Chapter 5

Around the County

Santa Monica

Although Santa Monica can trace its history back to Juan Rodriguez Cabrillo's 1542 exploration of the California coast and Gaspar de Portolà's 1769 overland expedition, for centuries there was little development of the beachfront community. The city's modern history began in earnest in 1872, when Colonel Robert S. Baker and his wife, Arcadia, purchased 38,409 acres of Rancho San Vicente y Santa Monica for the sum of $54,000. Two years later, Baker and another partner, Nevada senator John P. Jones, also purchased much of Rancho Boca de Santa Monica; the two former ranchos combined comprise modern Santa Monica.

In 1875, Baker and Jones began to design the layout of the town of Santa Monica. Many of the street names designated by these two men—includin the numbered streets and the state-named avenues—are still in use today. That same year, the first lots were sold and parks were established.

The year 1875 also saw the construction of the Los Angeles & Independence Railroad by Jones, Baker and others; this linked the infant Santa Monica to downtown Los Angeles. Built over the course of ten months and running almost seventeen miles, the railroad opened on October 17, 1875. Originally intended to continue to Independence, California, in Inyo County, the LA & Independence ran into trouble with the Southern Pacific regarding right-of-ways; money trouble also plagued the railroad, and in less than two years, it had been bought out by the Southern Pacific.

Tucked between apartments at 2621 Second Street in the Ocean Park neighborhood of Santa Monica is the city's oldest wooden building. The Methodist Episcopal Church has sat on the site since 1899, although its history can be traced back to the city's founding. In 1875, Senator Jones donated land at the corner of Sixth Street and Arizona Avenue for the city's first church. For a cost of $683.98, the congregation built, decorated and outfitted the Gothic Revival church itself. It opened its doors to the newly formed community on January 2, 1876.

As the years went on and the congregation grew, the church was moved around before arriving at its present location. By the 1920s, the building had been rebranded as a "patriotic hall" and was being used for meetings by such groups as the Grand Army of the Republic. Eventually, the building became a private residence and continues to give a glimpse at what Victorian Santa Monica would have been like.

While the Methodist Episcopal Church is the city's oldest wooden building, the title of oldest brick building goes to the Rapp Saloon (located at 1438 Second Street). Although there exists some discrepancy over whether the masonry building was constructed in 1873 or 1875, the saloon's long and storied history is undeniable. Having served as a beer garden, a city hall, an auto shop and headquarters for the Vitagraph Film Company, the building is now owned by Hosteling International and is used as a poetry reading space.

One local landmark from 1875 that is no longer standing was the "99 Steps," a wooden staircase located at the end of Arizona Boulevard that allowed residents and visitors access to the beach from up on the bluffs.

A little more than a decade later, the year 1886 saw the construction of Santa Monica's most opulent hotel and resort: the Arcadia. Named for Colonel Baker's wife, the Arcadia featured two hundred rooms situated on the bluffs overlooking the Pacific Ocean. Opened in January 1887, the $65,000 hotel was the second largest in Southern California behind the Raymond Hotel in Pasadena.

The Arcadia was unlike anything the Los Angeles area had ever seen before. A quintessentially Victorian beach resort, amenities included a bathhouse, a bowling alley, a billiards room and an observation tower that provided unobstructed views of the surrounding coastline. Perhaps the most unique feature was a gravity-powered roller coaster that took visitors on a journey to the beach and back for a nickel.

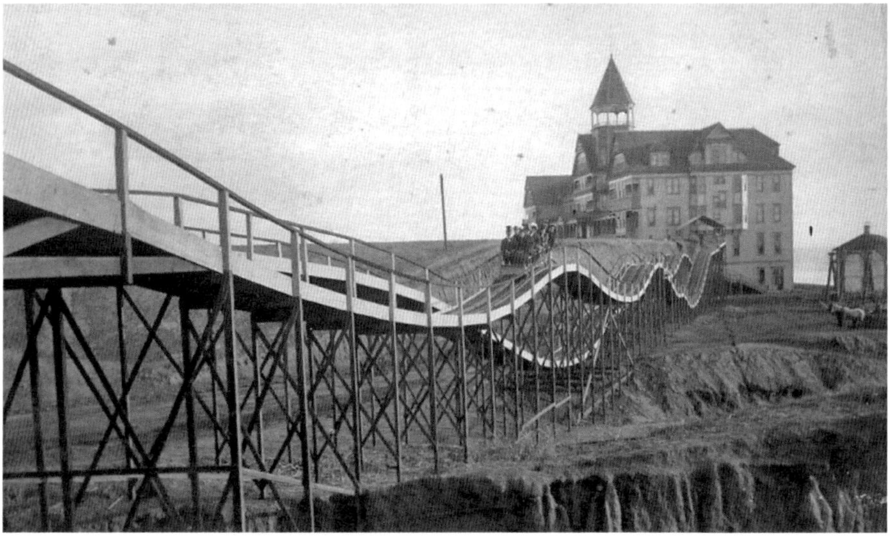

The Arcadia Hotel, opened in 1887, was at one time the second largest in Southern California. Not just a hotel, the resort featured bowling, billiards, an observation tower and a gravity-powered roller coaster that would take guests to the beach and back for a nickel. *Courtesy the Huntington Library.*

The Arcadia's reign as Southern California's most elegant beach resort was short-lived, however. The building's stately Victorian architecture was quickly looked upon as dated by many, and after only about a decade, the building lost much of its prestige. Despite the fanfare to which it opened, the Arcadia was unceremoniously demolished in 1909 to make way for a new housing project. Arcadia Terrace, located near the Santa Monica Pier, serves as a reminder to modern visitors of the Victorian resort that once was.

It is interesting to note how society's tastes have changed over the years. There was a time when, in addition to the Arcadia, there were multiple competitive beachside bathhouses, offering visitors an opportunity to swim indoors in heated water in addition to the ocean. Some, such as the North Beach Bath House, were elaborate structures that provided changing rooms, fresh- and saltwater plunges and other amenities. Today, Santa Monica's coast is bare of such structures, with visitors opting to simply swim in the ocean.

The year 1888 saw the construction of Senator Jones's mansion in Santa Monica. Named Miramar, meaning "sea view," the mansion was designed in a striking Victorian Shingle style that made it one of the most distinctive homes in the region. Turned into a hotel in 1924, the building was demolished in 1938. Although the site is now the Fairmont Miramar Hotel, there exists

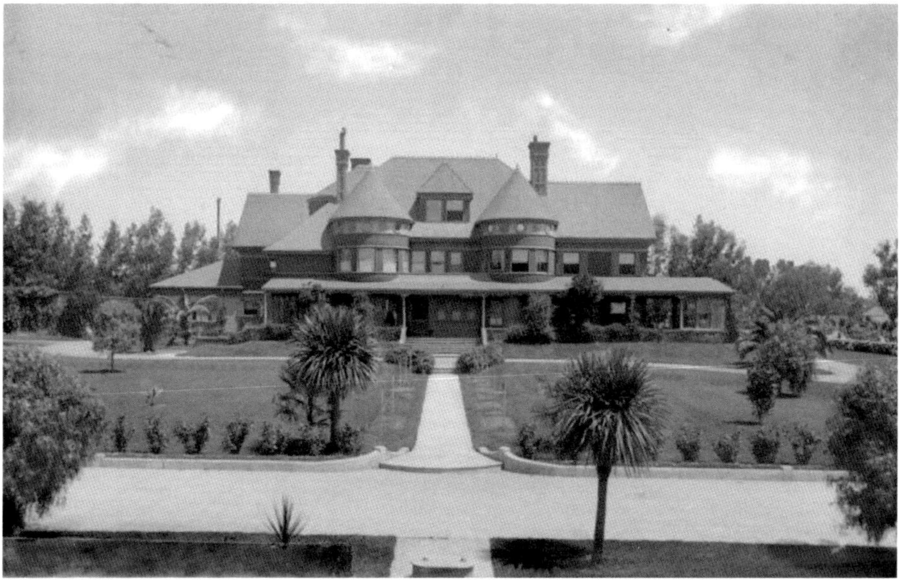

Senator John P. Jones's home, called Miramar ("sea view"), was one of the most distinctive Victorian homes in Santa Monica. It was converted into a hotel before being demolished in 1938, although a fig tree that once stood in front of the home still stands today. *Courtesy Water and Power Associates.*

one last remnant of Jones's home. In 1889, Jones's bartender gave him a Moreton Bay fig tree from Australia to plant in his yard. This tree still stands on the grounds of the Fairmont Miramar and is one of the largest such trees in the state of California.

In 1891, a man named Abbot Kinney purchased the Pacific Ocean Casino, located south of Santa Monica. Later that year, Kinney and his partner, Francis G. Ryan, also bought the stretch of beach from Strand Street to Brooks Avenue; after building a racetrack, a boardwalk and a golf course, Kinney renamed the property Ocean Park in 1895—the name that southern Santa Monica retains today. By 1905, the southern part of Kinney's property had been redeveloped and renamed the "Venice of America"; Venice's main thoroughfare is still named for Kinney.

By the 1890s, Santa Monica was putting pressure on San Pedro as Los Angeles's harbor. Between 1893 and 1894, the Southern Pacific Railroad constructed Long Wharf—the world's longest wharf, measuring 4,720 feet. Serviced by several local streetcar lines in addition to the Southern Pacific, Long Wharf was critical for the building boom of the 1890s, as one of its major imports was lumber from the Pacific Northwest.

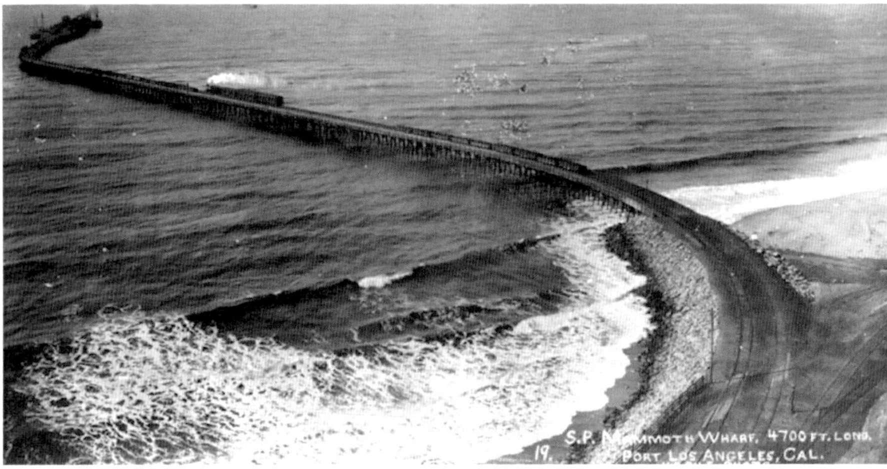

Santa Monica's "Long Wharf" was at one time the longest in the world, measuring more than 4,700 feet. During the 1890s, Santa Monica vied for the role of Los Angeles's port, although by the early 1900s, almost all commerce went through San Pedro. *Courtesy the Los Angeles Public Library.*

Throughout the 1890s, a bitter legal battle brewed between those who supported San Pedro as the region's main port and those who preferred Santa Monica. A major blow struck Long Wharf in 1899 when the federal government allocated funding for a breakwater at San Pedro—effectively eliminating Santa Monica's chance of success. Long Wharf continued to hang on until the 1910s, when demolition began. A segment of the wharf lingered as a fishing pier until 1933, when all traces were removed.

Today, California Historical Landmark #881 is located at the Will Rogers State Beach lifeguard headquarters, commemorating the site of what was once the world's longest pier. Although no trace remains, many houses constructed around the turn of the century are made of lumber that passed through Long Wharf.

One of Santa Monica's strangest landmarks still exists in an altered form. Built in 1898, the Camera Obscura was an octagonal building with a hole in the roof that allowed light into a darkened room. Similar to a pinhole camera, a periscope projected a 360-degree view of the surrounding beach onto a white board. Although moved to the top of the bluffs in 1907, the mechanism was moved to a nearby recreation center at 1450 Ocean Boulevard in 1951, where it continues to entertain today.

Santa Monica has changed dramatically since its early days as a quiet beach town. Although the city's original hotels and piers have been replaced, there is still a number of Victorian landmarks and homes that give a sense of what the city was like at the turn of the twentieth century—although some, like the Miramar fig tree or the Camera Obscura, require some digging into the city's history to realize their full significance.

PASADENA

Located in the San Gabriel Valley northeast of Los Angeles, the city of Pasadena can trace its heritage back to the Victorian era. Founded in 1874 and incorporated in 1886, Pasadena is the second-oldest city in the county, beating Santa Monica out by a matter of months.

Prior to its founding, the land that is now Pasadena was owned by Benjamin Wilson, a politician who was formerly the mayor of Los Angeles. In 1854, Wilson founded Lake Vineyard, his ranch and vineyard centered on a large, shallow lake. Wilson, who would lend his name to nearby Mount Wilson, lived in the vicinity until his death in 1878.

In 1873, a doctor from Indiana by the name of Daniel M. Berry traveled to Southern California in the hopes of finding a warmer climate for his respiratory patients, who had recently suffered the worst winter in the Midwest until that time. Various other communities were eliminated for a number of reasons, but Rancho San Pascual, near present-day Pasadena, proved perfect for his purposes.

By 1874, Dr. Berry had founded the Indiana Colony on the land that he and others purchased along the Arroyo Seco. Fair Oaks Boulevard, still a major thoroughfare today, was the dividing line between the Indiana Colony and Wilson's Lake Vineyard. Within a few years, however, the Indiana Colony name had been replaced by Pasadena—meaning "of the valley"—and the city began making strides toward incorporation. Wilson subdivided some of his remaining land to contribute to the city's development.

Pasadena was incorporated on June 19, 1886, just in time to benefit from the real estate boom of the 1880s. With the coming of the railroad that same decade, Pasadena quickly began blossoming into one of Southern California's premier resort destinations, and within a few years, hotels were opening at an unprecedented rate.

This growth was sparked, in large part, by Walter Raymond, who arrived in Pasadena in 1883. Recognizing Pasadena's potential as a railroad stop but noting that there were no hotels, he purchased a tract of land in Bacon

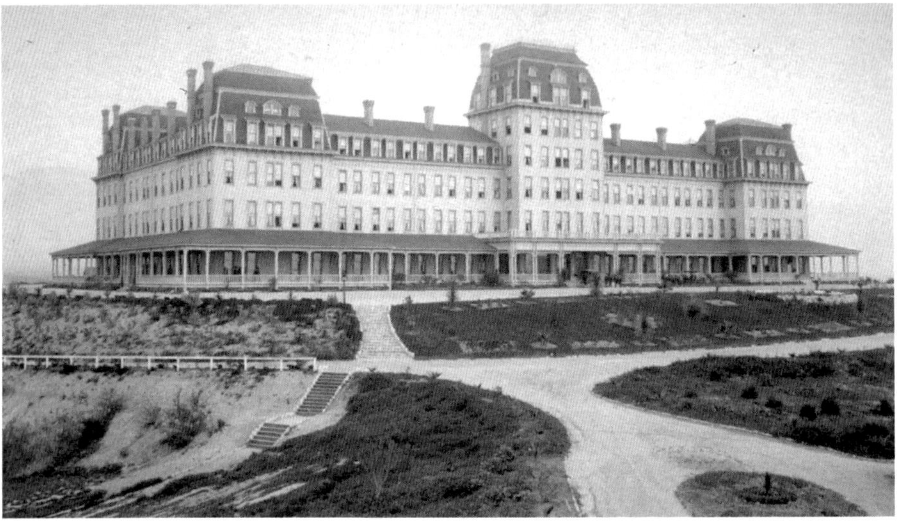

Pasadena's Raymond Hotel, opened in 1886, was at one time considered the premier hotel in the county. However, this building only stood for eight and a half years before a fire burned the entire structure to the ground. Today, the site of the hotel is still known as Raymond Hill. *Courtesy the University of California–Berkeley.*

Hill (later renamed Raymond Hill). With his father's fortune, he set out to build the luxurious Raymond Hotel. Today, Raymond Hill Road in South Pasadena still marks the location of the hotel. With two hundred rooms, the Raymond was the largest hotel in the Los Angeles and helped to establish the San Gabriel Valley as a resort destination.

The opening-night ball on November 17, 1886, was considered by some to be the most important social gathering in the history of the county. However, the stately Raymond Hotel stood for only eight and a half years before tragedy struck—the entire wooden structure burned to the ground on Easter morning in 1895. The hotel was rebuilt by 1901, although this time around, it lacked its distinctive Victorian architecture. The second Raymond Hotel was a victim of the Great Depression and was demolished during the 1930s.

Although short-lived, the Raymond Hotel solidified Pasadena's place as one of the county's major cities. Competitor hotels quickly began popping up after the success of the Raymond. One of the more notable of these was the Hotel Green, which was located at what is now the southeast corner of South Raymond Avenue and East Green Street.

Construction on the Hotel Green began in 1887 but was stalled due to financial issues. Colonel George Gill Green acquired the partially completed building and, after expanding it, opened the hotel in 1894. Considered the

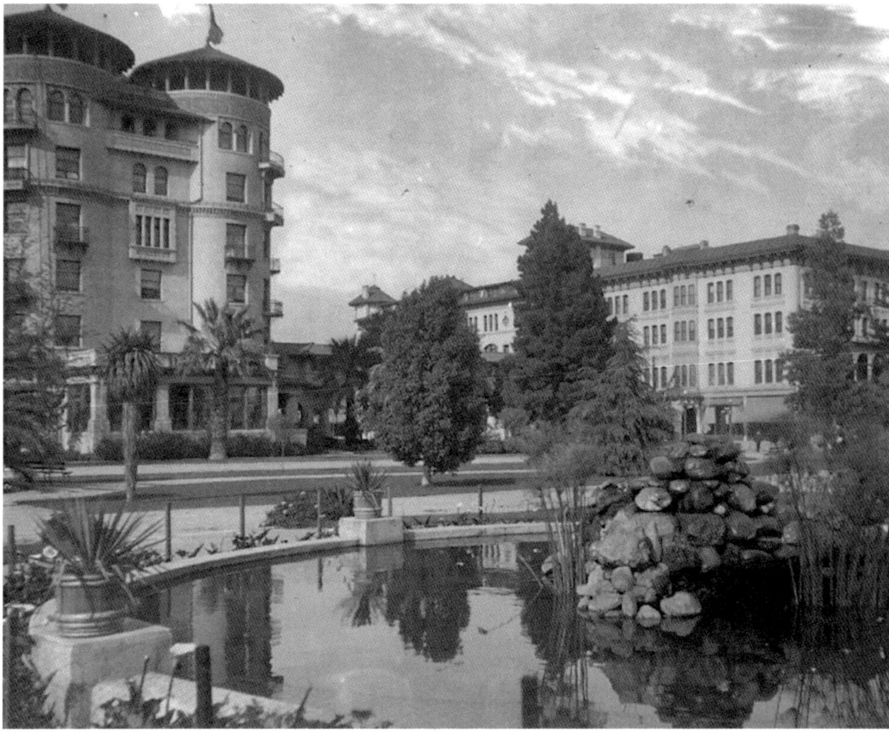

Another of Pasadena's grand Victorian hotels, the Hotel Green opened during the 1890s. It is notable for its distinctive architecture, which blends Mediterranean and Moorish influences. Today, portions of the former hotel have been converted into apartments. *Courtesy the Los Angeles Public Library.*

finest hotel in the city, a second building, the "Central Annex," was built between 1897 and 1899. A third addition, the Wooster Block (which earlier was the first home of Caltech), opened three years later in 1902.

Although the hotel suffered a decline in the 1910s and was converted into a private residence, the Central Annex—now known as Castle Green—managed to evade demolition and currently serves as an apartment complex. The seven-story building, designed by Frederick Roehrig, is one of the true Victorian architectural gems in the county. The Mediterranean style shows a heavy Moorish influence at a time when revival styles were beginning to take Southern California by storm.

Castle Green serves as a reminder of a time when Pasadena was a Victorian resort town, frequented by the wealthiest and most prominent locals and visitors. Numerous other hotels—such as La Pintoresca (the Painter), the Webster and the Carlton—contributed to create the resort character of this burgeoning city.

Not all of Pasadena's hotels were lost. The Evanston Inn (385–95 Marengo Avenue) is the city's only surviving wooden hotel. Constructed in 1897, the Evanston never had the prestige of Pasadena's more luxurious hotels, but its Queen Anne architecture makes it an integral part of the city's Victorian history.

Several modern Pasadena staples can trace their origins to the Victorian era. The *Pasadena Star-News*, for example, published its first issue in 1884, and Vroman's Bookstore opened its doors in 1894. Although both institutions have since moved from their original locations, they speak to the rich role that history plays in the community.

The California Institute of Technology, better known as Caltech, was also founded during Victorian times—although under a much different name. Amos Gager Throop, a politician, businessman and religious leader, established Throop University in 1891. Still in its infancy, the school rented rooms in the Wooster Block, an 1888 building at the corner of South Fair Oaks Boulevard and East Green Street. Rechristened Throop Polytechnic Institute two years later, it wouldn't be until 1920 that the current school's name came into usage.

Although Pasadena has made major strides to preserve its history, relatively few landmarks from the Victorian era still remain. The aforementioned Castle Green and Wooster Block stand out as two highlights. In the city's Old Town district, the Hotel Carver (107 South Fair Oaks Avenue) was constructed in about 1887 as a showroom for stagecoaches or carriages. Although having gone through numerous other iterations since then, the building has been renovated to meet earthquake safety regulations, and its brick façade is still remarkably well preserved.

Among Pasadena's Victorian homes, several stand out as architecturally significant. The Mary E. Denham House, located at 297 South Orange Grove Boulevard, was constructed in 1895 and shows a unique combination of Foursquare and Richardson Romanesque architectures. Hillmont, an 1887 home at 1375 East Mountain Street, is considered to be one of the finest Queen Anne homes in the entire city—rivaled by the 1893 Stoutenburgh House at 255 South Marengo Avenue. While by no means an exhaustive list, these three homes demonstrate the range of Victorian homes that can be found in Pasadena.

Pasadena has come along way since its humble founding in 1874. While no longer a resort destination located alongside the railroad tracks, with an economy based largely on tourism and hotels, there still exist many reminders of Pasadena's Victorian heritage. From its most famous school to its oldest newspaper and bookstore, many things that are quintessentially Pasadenan can trace their roots back to the earliest days of the city.

AVALON

Santa Catalina Island, located about twenty-two miles off the Southern California coast, is an incredibly popular tourist destination and serves as a convenient getaway for many Los Angeles residents. The island's history as a tourist resort can be traced all the way back to the 1880s, when steamboats began escorting passengers to the nearly barren harbor of Avalon.

The first steamer to make regular trips to the island was the SS *Amelia*, which ran from 1880 to 1883; however, it wasn't until George Shatto, a developer from Michigan, purchased the entire island for $200,000 in 1887 that the first makings of a resort community began. It was Shatto's sister-in-law who thought up the name Avalon for the island's main harbor, inspired by the fabled island of Avalon from Arthurian legend.

Almost as soon as Shatto bought the island, he began construction on the grand Hotel Metropole. Opened the following year, the Metropole occupied the site where a modern hotel of the same name currently stands. A three-story building, the hotel offered unobstructed views of the bay and dozens of rooms for visitors. Despite the hotel's grandeur and Shatto's vision for an island resort, his developments were a fiscal failure, and he was forced to sell the island within a few years.

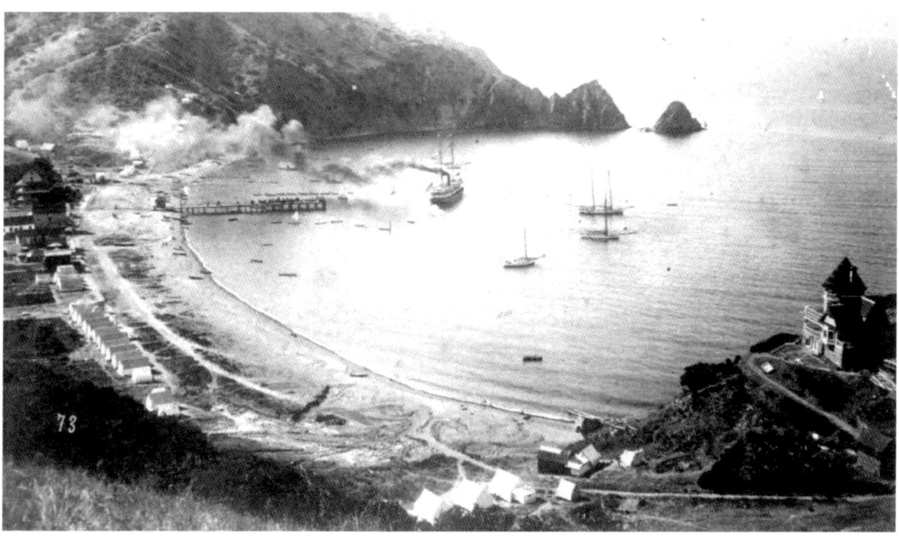

This late nineteenth-century view of Avalon Bay shows what the city looked like before the devastating fire of 1915. The Holly Hill House can be seen on the far right of the picture, while the Metropole Hotel is visible on the left. *Courtesy Water and Power Associates.*

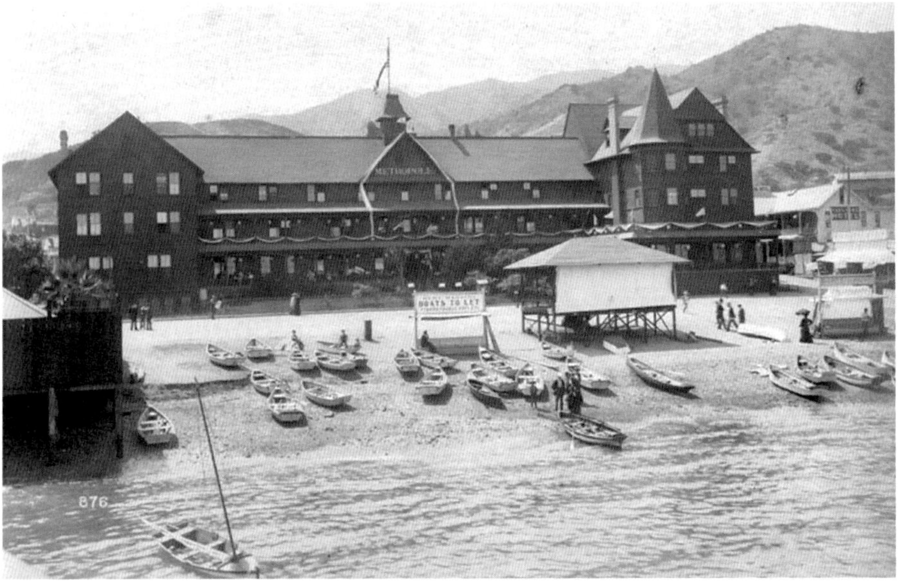

Not all grand Victorian hotels were confined to the mainland; Catalina Island's Hotel Metropole was considered to be one of the finest resorts in Southern California. As was the case with so many wooden buildings during this time, it burned to the ground in 1915. *Courtesy the Los Angeles Public Library.*

Catalina as it exists today came into being when Phineas Banning's sons purchased the island in 1891. Although the Banning family had been running the steamer *Hermosa* to the island under contract from Shatto, their primary reason for purchasing the island was practical: they needed a source for stone to construct the San Pedro breakwater.

The Bannings, however, also saw the potential for a tourist destination and continued to bring Shatto's dream to life. The Metropole was expanded in 1893 and 1897, with dozens of rooms and a large ballroom being added, and other amenities quickly began to spring up in Avalon. Many visitors elected to stay in tents that were pitched in the inland part of the city; soon thereafter, the Bannings began including free camping in the fare to travel to the island. This "tent city," although no longer present, was a very prominent landmark and can be seen in many early photos of the island.

The face of Avalon changed quickly during the first decades of the twentieth century. The Metropole burned to the ground in 1915, and once the island was acquired in large part by William Wrigley Jr. in 1919, widespread development began. Today, the only remnant of Victorian Avalon is the Holly Hill House, perched atop a hill overlooking the bay. Built in 1890, the home's Queen Anne architecture is dominated by a huge red- and green-striped conical roof that can be seen throughout Avalon.

An interesting legend exists about the man who constructed the home, Peter Gano. Gano built the house, which he called Lookout Cottage, for his fiancée; when she left him because of his desire to move to Avalon, he was so heartbroken that he posted "No Women Allowed" around his property.

LONG BEACH

Long Beach, by and large, was a city that boomed after the Victorian era had already ended. In fact, between 1902 and 1910, it was the fastest-growing city in the entire country, spurred in large part by improved transportation to and from Los Angeles. However, much of the infrastructure that led to Long Beach's rapid growth was laid out during the late nineteenth century, and that brief history will be recounted here.

In 1866, Rancho Los Cerritos (the former name of the Long Beach area) was placed under the management of Jothan Bixby—a man who

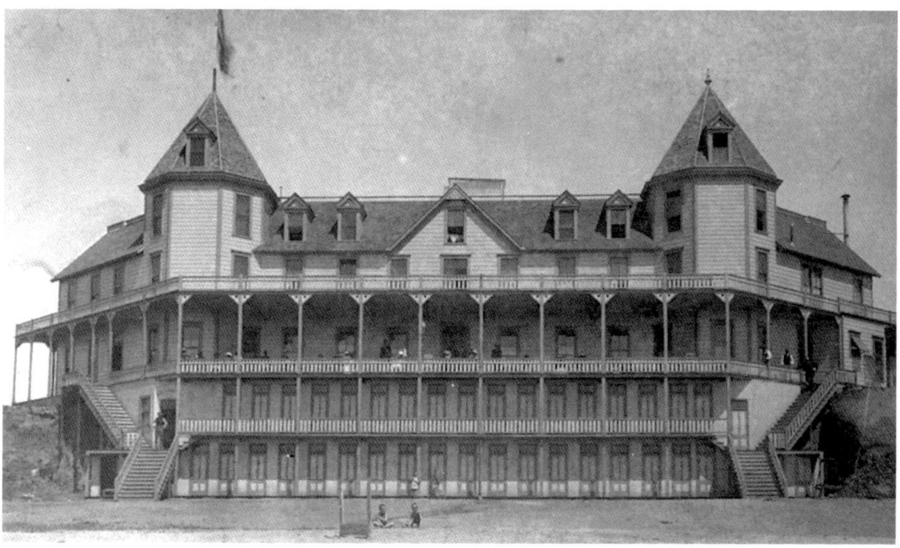

The Long Beach Hotel stood for only four years between 1884 and 1888, but it was significant for being a precursor to tourist attractions such as the Pike and Breakers Hotel during the first half of the twentieth century. The 130-room hotel featured an oceanfront dining room constructed entirely of glass. *Courtesy the Los Angeles Public Library.*

would become known as the "Father of Long Beach." Fourteen years later, in 1880, Bixby sold four thousand acres of land to William E. Willmore, who bought the land with the intention of starting a new community called Willmore City.

Despite a small housing boom in 1885, Willmore City never took off as envisioned, and Willmore was quickly bought out by the Los Angeles–based Long Beach Land and Water Company. It was this name, Long Beach, that residents began using to describe their community in about 1888.

Despite its fleeting existence, if not for the establishment of Willmore City, the history of Long Beach would be very different. Today, the Willmore City/Drake Park Historic District (centered on Seventh Street east of the Los Angeles River) preserves the city's former name and protects one of the oldest neighborhoods within Long Beach (although none of the homes dates back to the original settlement in the 1880s).

CHAPTER 6

VICTORIAN ATTRACTIONS

Some of the more unique features of Victorian Los Angeles were the curious attractions that developed around the county. While Los Angeles did have conventional forms of entertainment, like opera houses and theaters, there were also some nontraditional forms of recreation that would appear totally alien to a modern visitor.

BIRD FARMS

Although it may seem like a strange form of entertainment today, Southern California once boasted numerous ostrich farms. When put into context, however, it makes sense that these monstrous birds ended up in Los Angeles in such large numbers. During the 1880s, ostrich feathers were an incredibly popular fashion accessory, but importing them from Africa was cost-prohibitive for many. Entrepreneurial spirits quickly noticed the potential for raising the feathers much closer to the American markets, and quickly a steady stream of ostriches was making the long boat ride across the Atlantic.

Of all of Los Angeles's ostrich farms, the most famous was the Cawston Ostrich Farm, which was originally located in Norwalk for the first ten years of its existence. Although Edwin Cawston shipped fifty ostriches from Africa in 1886, only eighteen survived the strenuous trip. Fortunately, ostriches

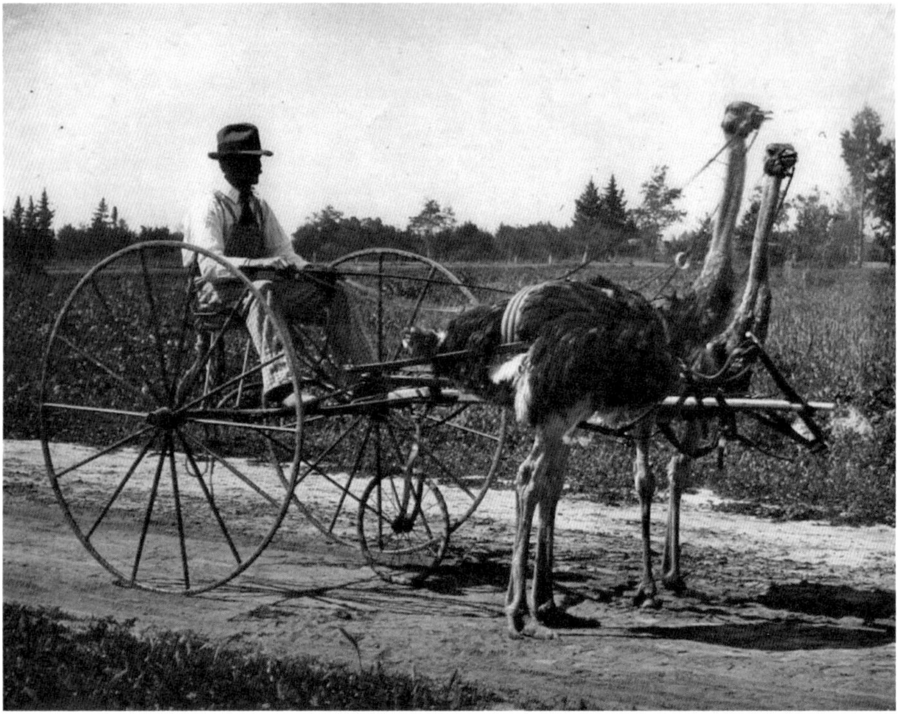

Two ostriches pull a man in a cart at Cawston Ostrich Farm, one of the most unique attractions in Victorian Los Angeles. Visitors were able to purchase souvenirs made out of ostrich feathers, a valuable commodity during the late nineteenth century. *Courtesy the South Pasadena Public Library.*

prospered in the Southern California climate, and within several years, his flock had considerably multiplied. In 1895, he moved his farm to 1010 Sycamore Avenue in South Pasadena, where his birds would continue to entertain guests until 1935.

At the Cawston Ostrich Farm, visitors were able to take ostrich rides (either on the animal's back or in a carriage), while also being able to purchase a number of ostrich souvenirs plucked right at the farm. Boas, hats and fans were all incredibly fashionable during the late Victorian era, and the fact that feathers no longer had to be shipped in from so far away expanded the demographic of women who were able to own these items.

Ostrich feathers had gone out of style by the 1910s, although the farm continued to prosper until the Great Depression. Although the idea of an ostrich farm in a major metropolis seems unfathomable today, Cawston's (and others) served a practical purpose, as well as being popular forms of

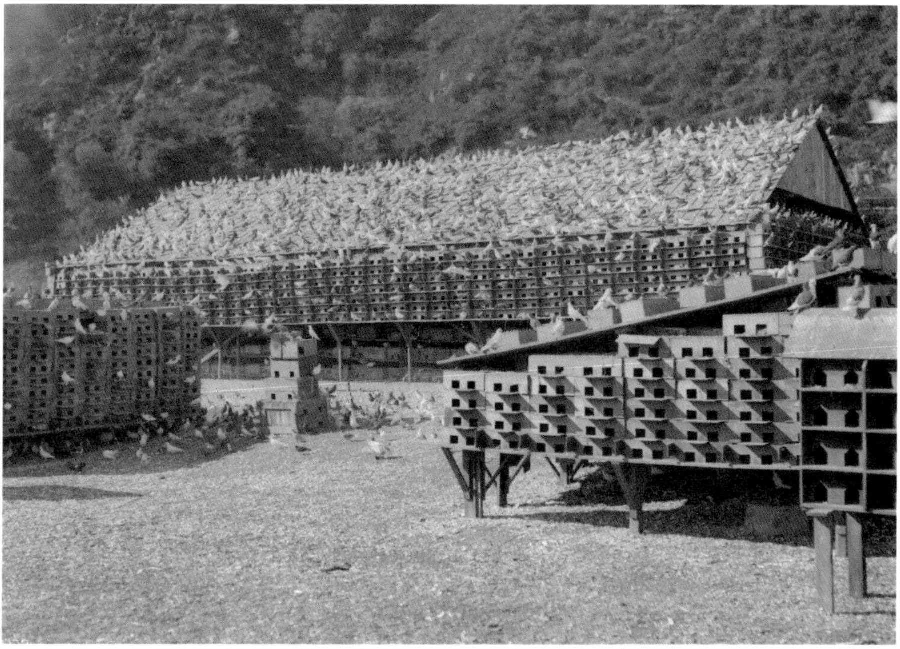

The Los Angeles Pigeon Farm was at one time the largest in the world, with more than 100,000 birds held in captivity. The spectacle of so many pigeons made it a local curiosity that many people visited during its brief history. *Courtesy California Historical Society.*

entertainment. Although long gone, one of the original brick buildings from the Cawston Farm is still standing, fittingly renamed the Ostrich Farm Lofts.

Ostriches were not the only birds that were tourist attractions in Victorian Los Angeles. There was, very briefly, also a pigeon farm in the city at a time when squab meat was very highly prized. Opened in 1892 near Elysian Park, the pigeon farm was not intended as a tourist attraction at first, but the thousands of birds were such a strange sight that it was inevitable that people would visit.

At its peak, the Los Angeles Pigeon Farm was said to be the largest in the world, with more than 100,000 birds. Feeding time was a daily attraction—each day, more than two tons of grain were consumed. However, the pigeon farm proved not to be as long-lived as the ostrich farm; in 1914, a rainstorm caused flooding that killed most of the farm's birds, with the survivors being released into the wild.

CHUTES PARK

Although not established until the very end of the Victorian era, Chutes Park was Los Angeles's nearest approximation of a Victorian pleasure garden and trolley park. During the earliest days of streetcars and trolleys, opportunistic developers would often create small parks, sometimes with a pavilion or bandstand, at the end of their lines. Chutes Park, which went by numerous names over the course of its brief history, was one such park, founded in 1887.

It wasn't until 1899 that Chutes Park began to develop into a full-blown amusement park. Under new ownership, a complete renovation of the property was begun. By 1900, a baseball stadium had been added, and plans were drawn up for a number of rides and attractions. Foremost among the attractions was Paul Boyton's Shoot the Chutes ride, a water ride consisting of a seventy-five-foot drop (similar to one he had opened at Coney Island). Boyton was a popular showman famous for popularizing water sports across the world.

Around the same time that the Shoot the Chutes ride was added, Chutes Park also constructed the Chutes Theater (a vaudeville venue), as well as a fishing pond, hot air balloon rides and other novelties for people to enjoy.

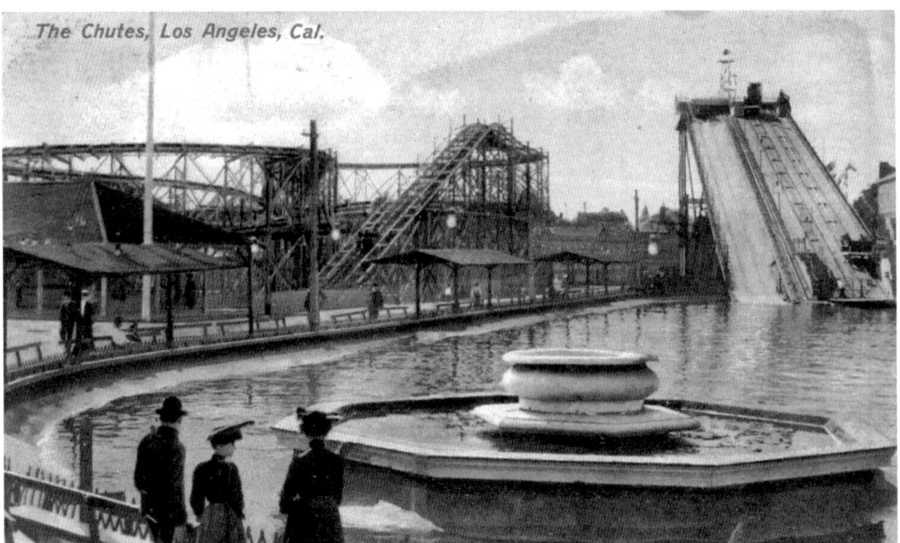

Decades before Disneyland or Knott's Berry Farm, Chutes Park was Los Angeles's first prototypical amusement park. The most major attraction, seen in the right of this postcard, was a "Shoot the Chutes" ride featuring a seventy-five-foot drop. *Courtesy Loyola Marymount University.*

Several animals were exhibited, including a vampire bat—a rare sight for city dwellers at that time.

Despite the potential for an amusement park near downtown Los Angeles, the park was never lucrative for its owners. In 1910, Chutes Park underwent a major overhaul and rebranding, and the following year, it was reopened as Luna Park (named after the amusement park at Coney Island). Luna Park experienced an even shorter lifespan than Chutes Park, closing for good in 1914.

The location of Chutes Park—bounded by Grand Avenue, Main Street, Washington Boulevard, and Twenty-first Street just south of downtown—is today home to a courthouse and several commercial buildings. However, while short-lived and largely unsuccessful, Chutes Park does have the distinction of being Southern California's first amusement park, decades before Knott's Berry Farm and Disneyland were created. For this reason alone, it serves as a crucial part of Los Angeles's history and depicts an era that was very fleeting in this part of the nation.

Mount Lowe Railway

Another of Victorian Los Angeles's unique attractions was the Mount Lowe Railway, a scenic electric trolley that took passengers up Echo Mountain and Mount Lowe in the San Gabriel Mountains. The railway, and its remnants today, have been written about extensively, and what follows is only a brief history of the line.

The Mount Lowe Railway was the product of a meeting between two men—David J. Macpherson, a civil engineer who served as the brains behind the operation, and Professor Thaddeus S.C. Lowe, a millionaire who provided the funds that Macpherson needed. In 1891, they incorporated the Pasadena & Mount Wilson Railroad Company but, unable to acquire a right-of-way to the top of Mount Wilson, were quickly forced to look into other options for their scenic mountain railway. They settled for Mount Lowe (named after Professor Lowe), a less prominent peak nearby.

Work was finally begun on the railroad in 1892. The route to the foot of Mount Lowe was divided into three segments: the Mountain Division, the Great Incline and the Alpine Division. The Mountain Division began in Altadena and terminated in Rubio Canyon, where travelers were met with the Rubio Pavilion—a twelve-room hotel that featured walking trails around the canyon, a dining room and other conveniences.

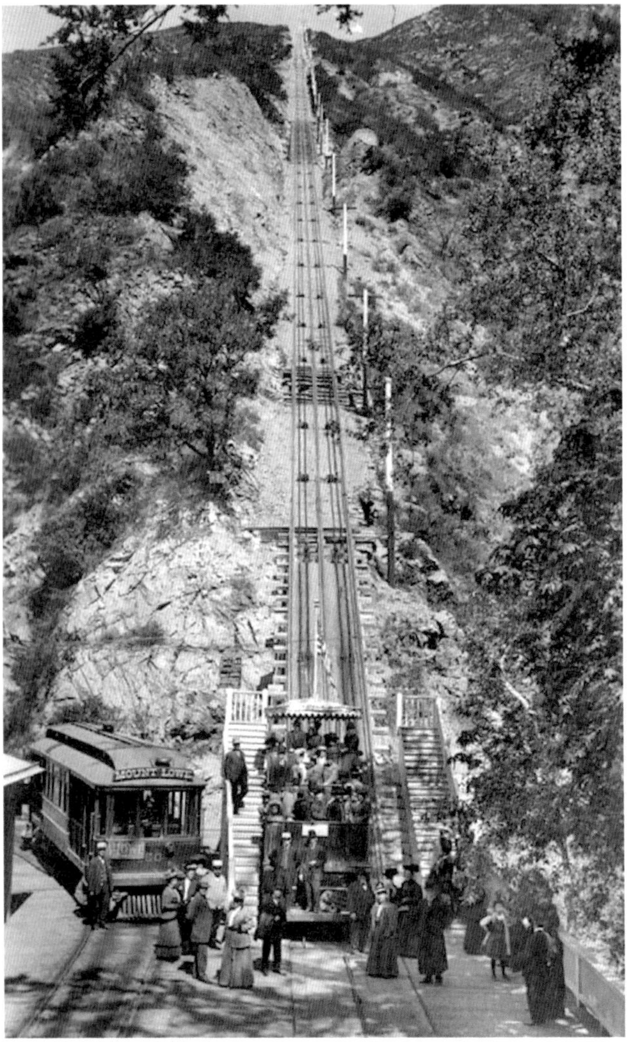

The segment of the Mount Lowe Railway known as the "Great Incline" was one of the most impressive engineering feats in Los Angeles until that time. Rising 2,200 feet at a grade as steep as 62 percent, traces of the track can still be found by hikers in the area today. *Courtesy the Los Angeles Public Library.*

Seeking to provide his guests with an immersive experience, Lowe went as far as to name the individual waterfalls in Rubio Canyon and provided viewing platforms. These waterfalls—featuring such picturesque names as Maidenhair Falls, Moss Grotto Falls, and Roaring Rift Falls—are still accessible to hikers today.

Rising from Rubio Pavilion was the Great Incline, arguably one of the most impressive engineering feats of its day. Rising 2,200 feet at a grade as steep as 62 percent, the design of this stretch of the railroad was so innovative that it would influence the construction of future funicular railroads (such as

Los Angeles's Angels Flight). The mountainside on which the Great Incline was built was so steep that mules refused to climb up it; instead, construction materials had to be carried up on the backs of workers.

The Great Incline ended at the summit of Echo Mountain, which served as a resort getaway for many locals. When the railroad opened on July 4, 1893, passengers were greeted by the forty-room Echo Chalet; it wasn't until late the following year that the Echo Mountain House, twice the size of the chalet and much more luxurious, was ready for guests.

The Echo Mountain House, one of the most lavish hotels in Southern California, was not the only attraction awaiting travelers. During the last years of the nineteenth century, Echo Mountain also featured a small zoo, a telescope and a three-million-candlepower searchlight that was purchased when the Columbian Exposition in Chicago closed in 1893. The light was so powerful that it had a range of thirty-five miles and could pick out individual houses throughout the Los Angeles Basin. Because all of the buildings at the summit of Echo Mountain were painted stark white, the resort quickly became known as "the White City in the sky" (no doubt a reference to the Columbian Exposition).

The third section of track, constructed between 1894 and 1896, was known as the Alpine Division. Crossing three canyons and again featuring

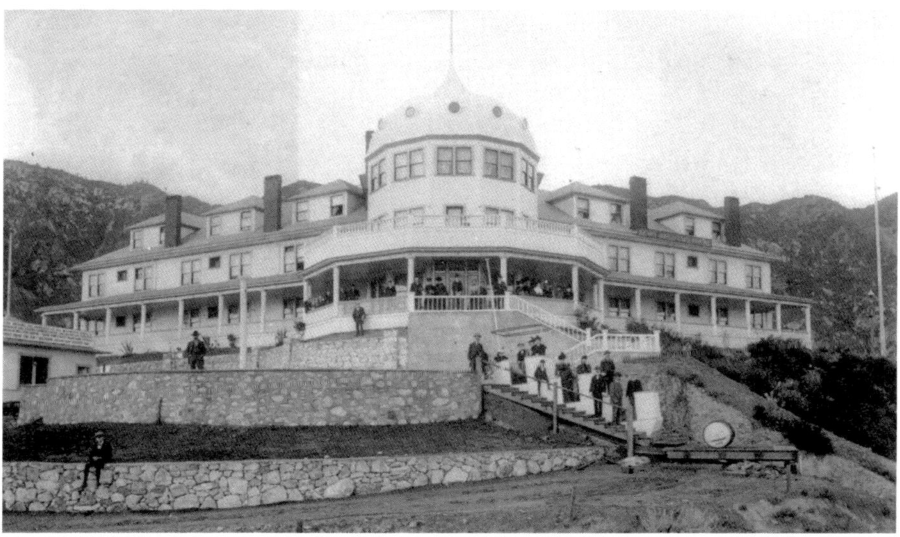

The Echo Mountain House, located midway up the Mount Lowe Scenic Railway, was a lavish eighty-room hotel. The Echo Mountain House was only open for about six years before a fire destroyed the resort. *Courtesy the Los Angeles Public Library.*

spectacular feats of engineering (courtesy of Macpherson), the Alpine Division terminated at Ye Alpine Tavern, a twelve-room Swiss Chalet.

Tragedy struck the Mount Lowe Railway in 1900, when a fire burned the Echo Mountain House to the ground; several additional fires over the next few decades would prove equally disastrous. Despite attempts to rehabilitate and reconstruct the buildings along the line, the railway would make its final trip in December 1937. Following extensive flooding the next year, the line was officially abandoned; during World War II, all remaining usable material was salvaged.

Beginning in the early 1990s, the historical significance of the Mount Lowe Railway was realized, and today the Scenic Mount Lowe Railway Historical Committee continues to work to preserve artifacts and inform visitors to the area about the line's significance. Hikers today can still find traces of the Great Incline, the Echo Mountain House and other features of the railway, fleeting reminders of one of Los Angeles's first true tourist attractions.

CHAVEZ RAVINE ARBORETUM

Not every Victorian attraction has vanished; some, such as the Chavez Ravine Arboretum (929 Academy Road), still delight visitors to this day. Founded in 1893 by the Los Angeles Horticultural Society, the Chavez Ravine Arboretum was the first of its kind in Southern California, predating the Los Angeles County Arboretum by half a century.

The Horticultural Society continued planting rare trees in the park well into the 1920s; a majority of these original trees are still standing today. According to the City of Los Angeles Department of Recreation and Parks, which runs the site today, "many of the trees are the oldest and largest of their kind in California and even the United States."

Protected as a Historic-Cultural Monument since 1967, the Chavez Ravine Arboretum is free and open to the public daily, carrying on the legacy of what was first begun during the Victorian era.

ANGELS FLIGHT

Constructed at the very end of the Victorian era proper, Angels Flight is one of Los Angeles's most important and recognizable links to the turn of the

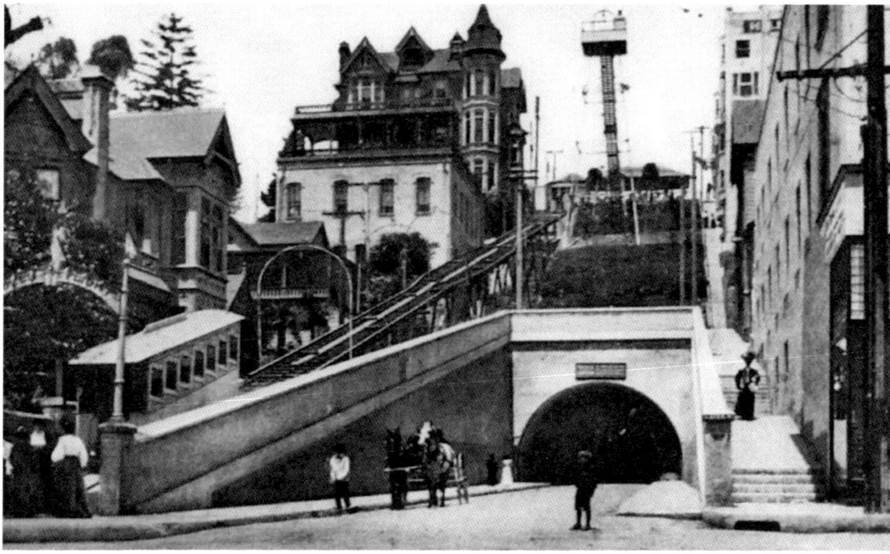

An early view of Angels Flight at its original location. Today, Angels Flight stands a half block away from where it originally ran due to development in the 1960s. Although plagued by several accidents over its long history, Angels Flight is Southern California's last remaining funicular railroad. *Courtesy the Los Angeles Public Library.*

twentieth century. Although Southern California was once home to several incline railways, Angels Flight is the last of these remaining. Angels Flight has also claimed, at various points in its history, to be the shortest incorporated railroad in the world, as well as having carried more passengers than any other railway.

Angels Flight was constructed in 1901 by Colonel J.W. Eddy, a former friend of Abraham Lincoln who financed the railroad without any public support. One station was located on the southwest corner of Hill and Third Streets, while the other was on top of Bunker Hill (where Eddy lived) at Olive Street.

Two cars—named "Olivet" and "Sinai"—carried riders up and down the hill using a gravity-powered system; when one car was on its way up, the other was traveling down the hill to the Hill Street station. A three-rail system, developed during the construction of the Mount Lowe Railway's Great Incline, was utilized by Angels Flight. The track was 315 feet long and ran at a 33 percent grade. When it first opened, the one-minute ride cost passengers one penny.

By the 1950s, Bunker Hill was in the midst of a major redevelopment, and the future of Angels Flight looked grim. Fortunately, in 1962, the Cultural

Heritage Board declared the railway one of the city's first five Historic-Cultural Monuments; when Angels Flight was closed seven years later, the cars, track and stations were all placed in storage.

It wouldn't be until twenty-seven years later that Angels Flight would once again see the light of day. A half block from its original site, the new Angeles Flight used new track but the original two cars, "Olivet" and "Sinai." Since its reinstallation, there have been several serious accidents on the line, and as of this writing, Angels Flight is closed for an unspecified amount of time.

Despite it currently being out of commission, the fact that Angels Flight still exists at all is a testament to the preservation movement in Los Angeles. While many other landmarks from the late Victorian era have been lost over the intervening century, Angels Flight fortunately still harkens back to a time when Los Angeles was immeasurably different.

HAZARD'S PAVILION

Victorian Los Angeles's most prominent entertainment venue was undoubtedly Hazard's Pavilion, a large auditorium located on the northeast corner of Olive and Fifth Streets (now a parking lot). Opened in April 1887, Hazard's Pavilion (named after then city attorney Henry Hazard) seated four thousand and quickly became a venue for all sorts of events. Everything from religious meetings to boxing matches to operas were held there on a regular basis.

The era's biggest names made appearances at Hazard's Pavilion while they were in Los Angeles. Everyone from President Benjamin Harrison to William Jennings Bryan to Booker T. Washington made speeches. An up-and-coming Enrico Caruso once sang at Hazard's. And a young Jim Jeffries, raised in Los Angeles, appeared in his only recorded local fight there. During the late nineteenth century, Hazard's Pavilion was the only venue in Los Angeles that could accommodate such notable events.

By 1906, the city had outgrown the pavilion, which also exhibited dated Victorian-style architecture that was frowned upon. A new building, Clune's Auditorium (later the Philharmonic Auditorium), was quickly constructed on the same site. A notable building in its own right, Clune's Auditorium was the site of the premiere of D.W. Griffith's classic *Birth of a Nation.*

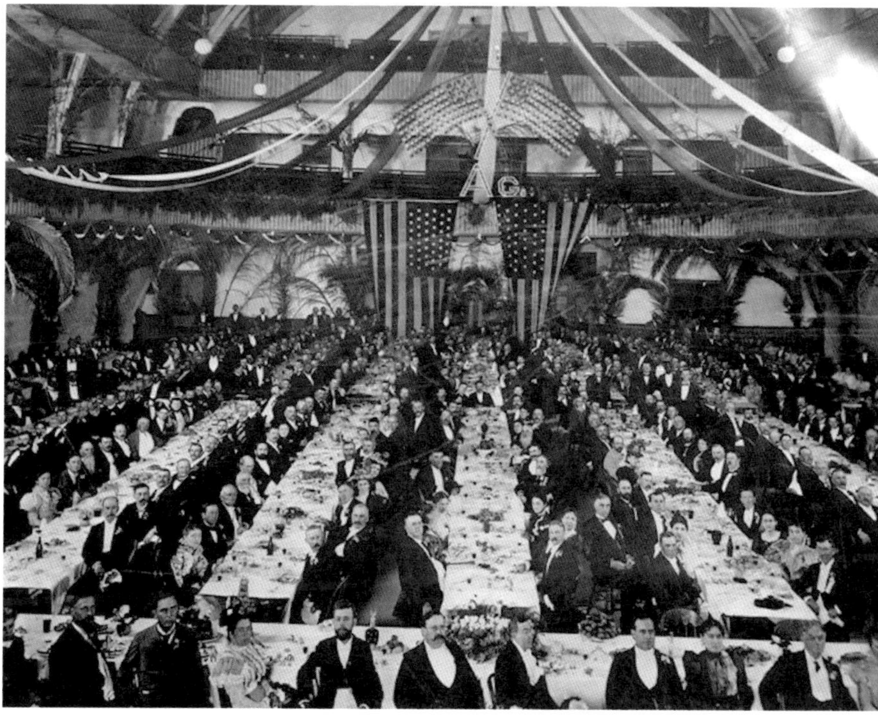

In 1897, William Jennings Bryan spoke at Hazard's Pavilion. Built in 1887, it was the largest venue in Los Angeles at the time. Before its demolition in 1906, Hazard's Pavilion also hosted Enrico Caruso, Carrie Nation and Booker T. Washington. *Courtesy the Los Angeles Public Library.*

Although no trace of Hazard's Pavilion exists today, it is important to remember the critical role that it played in providing world leaders with a place to appear in Los Angeles as the city was first starting to develop into a cultural hub. Such events helped to solidify the city as one of the West's major metropolitan centers.

CHAPTER 7

TRACES OF VICTORIAN LOS ANGELES

Neighborhoods and Homes

The next three chapters are all related—they describe traces of Victorian Los Angeles that still exist today. Sites are divided into three categories: residential neighborhoods and buildings, the historic core of downtown Los Angeles and designated historic parks. These chapters are not intended to be exhaustive lists of all remaining structures from the Victorian era; instead, they simply serve as representative guides of what are generally considered to be the most significant surviving buildings from the nineteenth century.

VICTORIAN NEIGHBORHOODS

For all of the development that the city underwent during the twentieth century, Los Angeles is still very fortunate to have several neighborhoods composed primarily of Victorian homes. While a lone home from the late nineteenth century is often an impressive sight, it is nothing compared to setting foot on a street lined with Queen Anne houses. When imagining what life was like in Los Angeles during the Victorian era, it is important to have a fully immersive experience, and while it is impossible to imagine how Bunker Hill once looked, overflowing with architectural wonders, the following four neighborhoods are about as close as one can get today to traveling back in time to the nineteenth century.

Angelino Heights

When most people in Los Angeles think of Victorian homes, they think of Angelino Heights—and rightfully so. The Echo Park neighborhood has an incredibly dense concentration of architecturally significant homes, a number of which were designed in the Queen Anne and Eastlake styles. Some historians suggest that Angelino Heights may have the highest concentration of Victorian homes in the entire county.

Within Angelino Heights, the 1300 block of Carroll Avenue in particular has been federally registered as a historical site due to the incredibly well-preserved nature of its homes; twelve homes on this block are further recognized as Los Angeles Historic-Cultural Monuments. The fact that the entire block, and several surrounding streets, is crowded with solely Victorian homes is fairly unique in the city; most neighborhoods feature eclectic mixtures of architectural styles as they developed over the decades.

In 1983, Angelino Heights became Los Angeles's first Historic Preservation Overlay Zone, ensuring that none of the homes in the district would be extensively remodeled and requiring that all new construction preserves the architectural integrity of the neighborhood.

Angelino Heights began during the building boom of the 1880s, when Los Angeles's population was exploding and construction ran wild. As one of Los Angeles's first real suburbs, development peaked in about 1887. A lull in the economy several years later meant a gap in the construction of homes until the early 1900s—leaving the perfectly preserved Victorian neighborhood at the core of Angelino Heights.

William W. Stilson and Everett E. Hall were the two men responsible for the founding of Angelino Heights in 1886, and almost immediately lots began selling for $500 each. The addition of the horse-drawn Temple Street Cable Railway, which connected the suburb to downtown, helped sales greatly. Although construction quickly came to a stop in 1888, no fewer than fifty-one homes had already been completed, with many still standing today.

There are enough historic homes in Angelino Heights to warrant a book of their own, and the Los Angeles Conservancy offers walking tours that detail the neighborhood's history and chronology. Because of the sheer scope of the neighborhood, only a few homes will be mentioned by name; however, this is not to disparage any of the other exceptional houses in the neighborhood, all of which could rightfully have been included.

The Eastlake-style Innes House (1329 Carroll Avenue), built in 1887, was one of the first homes on Carroll Avenue to receive specific historic designation from the city. Built the same year but representing a different facet of Victorian architecture is the Scheerer House (1324 Carroll Avenue), which is a prototypical prefabricated home from the 1880s. During this time, it was not unusual to mail-order a home from a catalogue such as Montgomery Ward of Sears, Roebuck.

One of the later Victorian homes to be built in Angelino Heights was the Haskins House (1344 Carroll Avenue), erected by a local real estate agent in the mid-1890s. Nicknamed the "Gay Nineties" house, the Haskins Residence represents a later, more ornamental Victorian architectural style than its neighbors.

Other Victorian homes have since been moved to Angelino Heights from elsewhere in the city. One such house is Samuel Foy Residence (1337 Carroll Avenue), originally located at Figueroa and Seventh Streets downtown. Built in 1872 in an Italianate style, it has been saved from demolition several times by preservationists and is currently one of the oldest houses left in Los Angeles.

South Bonnie Brae Tract Historic District

Tucked near the intersection of the 110 and 10 Freeways, not far south of MacArthur Park, is the South Bonnie Brae Tract Historic District. While the neighborhood lacks the fanfare of Angelino Heights and West Adams, it is one of the best-preserved Victorian streets in the entire city. Somehow, despite development on all sides, this entire segment of South Bonnie Brae Street has managed to slip through the cracks and remains incredibly pristine today.

Running intermittently between Washington Boulevard and Sunset Boulevard, the interestingly named Bonnie Brae Street (which means "pleasant hill" in Gaelic) can trace its origins back to at least the 1880s—about a decade before many of the houses along the 1000 block of South Bonnie Brae were constructed. Additionally, three houses on the street were constructed in about 1890 on the 1000 block of South Olive Street and later moved to Bonnie Brae in 1909.

What makes the homes in the Bonnie Brae tract so important is that they straddle the line between Queen Anne and Colonial Revival architecture. As the nineteenth century was coming to a close, Queen Anne architecture quickly began to fade—particularly in Southern California, where a multitude of other styles began to flourish. Within a few decades, new homes were increasingly designed in Craftsman, Colonial Revival, Mission

Revival or other relatively new styles. Bonnie Brae represents one of the last strongholds of typical Victorian architecture in Los Angeles.

Spurred by the development of nearby streetcar lines, much of the Pico-Union neighborhood was surveyed during the 1890s as the land surrounding downtown was being converted to suburbs. Today, the sixteen homes that compose the South Bonnie Brae Tract Historic District give a unique glimpse into what suburban life would have been like as the Victorian era came to a close.

One house in the historic district is separately listed as a Los Angeles Historic-Cultural Monument. The residence at 1036 South Bonnie Brae Street, known as the Marley-Stone House, is one of the few surviving examples of Châteauesque architecture in Los Angeles. Châteauesque—or Château style—was inspired by French Renaissance architecture and was one of a multitude of revival styles to crop up during the Victorian period. Built in 1896, the Marley-Stone House features twin turrets, intricate woodwork, stained-glass windows and classical columns. The minute details of the house's façade help it to stand out as a true architectural masterpiece.

North University Park Historic District

Located just north of the University of Southern California's campus is the North University Park Historic District, one of several historically designated neighborhoods in the area. Many of the district's homes are textbook examples of Victorian and Craftsman architecture, with several dating back to the 1880s (not long after the university itself was founded and the area began to flourish).

Land was subdivided into housing plots beginning in 1885; when USC was founded in 1880, much of the surrounding land was sold to raise funds, which brought in prominent investors and developers. Early on, many wealthy Los Angeles businessmen and politicians, as well as professors from USC, moved into the region. By 1888, homes were selling for $3,000. Streetcars linked the North University Park neighborhood to downtown in 1891, prompting a boom in growth over the next decade.

Almost certainly the oldest house in North University Park is the Forthmann House (2801 South Hoover Boulevard). Currently the sixth-oldest home in Los Angeles, it was built about one mile from its current location in 1887. John A. Forthmann, a German soap manufacturer, commissioned Burgess J. Reeve to design the Victorian mansion, which is a mixture of many styles, including Eastlake and Italianate. In 1989, the house was relocated to its current location at 2801 South Hoover Boulevard to prevent its destruction during the building of the new Los Angeles Convention Center. Along the way, streetlamps had to be removed, as the house was too wide, and it was actually cheaper to replace the lamps than to modify the house.

Nearby is another of the neighborhood's earliest home, the Miller and Herriott House (1163 West Twenty-seventh Street), constructed in 1890. A combination of the Stick and Eastlake Victorian styles of architecture, this house is particularly interesting because when the land was originally being settled, developers used it as the model home to attract buyers to the neighborhood. Today, the home is used as housing for USC students.

The William W. Cockins House (2653 South Hoover Street) is a late Queen Anne–style home that is heralded by architects as one of the finest examples of the style in the city. Built in 1894, it was converted to a boardinghouse not long after its construction. Allegedly, Charlie Chaplin rented a room in this home when he moved to Los Angeles for the first time in 1913; there's even a mannequin of his Tramp character on the second-story balcony.

Although the Victorian homes located in North University Park are too numerous to cover in detail in this book, others that deserve special mention include the Ibbetson House (1190 West Adams Boulevard), which combines traditional Victorian architecture with the relatively rare Richardsonian Romanesque style, as well as the Salisbury House (2703 South Hoover Street), a classic example of Queen Anne architecture that is representative of the style at its peak in Los Angeles.

Heritage Square Museum

Although not a neighborhood per se, Montecito Heights's Heritage Square Museum (3800 Homer Street) is a dream come true for any fan of the Victorian era. Founded in 1969, the "museum" is unconventional in that it is a collection of buildings that were moved to the property in order to save them from demolition. During the 1960s, when historic structures were being lost at an unprecedented rate, the Heritage Square Museum was created as a repository for some of the city's finest (and most endangered) Victorian buildings.

Today, the museum contains five Victorian-era houses, preserved and restored, alongside a carriage barn, a train depot and a church that all date from this period. With its mission to preserve the decades following

California's statehood, there is perhaps no better place in the county to immerse oneself in the late nineteenth century. Guided tours each weekend provide visitors with a remarkable view of Victorian Los Angeles.

The oldest building on the property, the William Hayes Perry Residence, is also considered to be the oldest mansion in Los Angeles. Perry, who had the home constructed in 1876 in Boyle Heights, was a very prominent lumber baron during the second half of the nineteenth century. Also known as the Mount Pleasant House, the Perry Mansion is the largest home at the Heritage Square Museum. It was designed by E.F. Kysor, who was once described as "one of Los Angeles's most prominent architects" and was also responsible for USC's first building. Designed in a striking Greek Revival Italianate style, the Perry Mansion was saved from demolition by the National Society of the Colonial Dames of America and moved to Heritage Square in 1975.

Built only slightly later than the Perry Mansion is the Shaw House, also called the Valley Knudsen Garden-Residence. Built sometime around 1880 in East Los Angeles, the home is most remarkable for its architectural style, which is a rare example of French Second Empire. Second Empire, with its characteristic mansard roof, was never particularly popular in California; however, the fact that the Shaw House was built at such a late date makes it even more remarkable.

Rounding out Heritage Square's Victorian homes are the circa 1885 Ford House, which features ornate hand-carved woodwork from original owner, John J. Ford, and the Hale House, an imposing example of Queen Anne and Eastlake Victorian architectures. The latest home at the museum is also the most architecturally unique—the Longfellow-Hastings "Octagon" House. Constructed in 1893, it is one of the only surviving octagonal houses left in the western United States; there are only about five hundred left in the entire country.

Also at the Heritage Square Museum is an 1899 carriage barn relocated from Pasadena, as well as the Lincoln Avenue Methodist Church, which was constructed between 1897 and 1898. Both buildings exemplify the Queen Anne style, with the latter also showing a strong Carpenter Gothic influence in its architecture.

The last of the Victorian buildings at Heritage Square is the Palms Railroad Depot. When the Los Angeles & Independence Railroad opened in the 1870s, "Bay View" was one of only two stops between Santa Monica and downtown. Renamed Palms in 1886, when construction of the depot started, the area also had another nickname due to unwanted pests: "Grasshopper Stop."

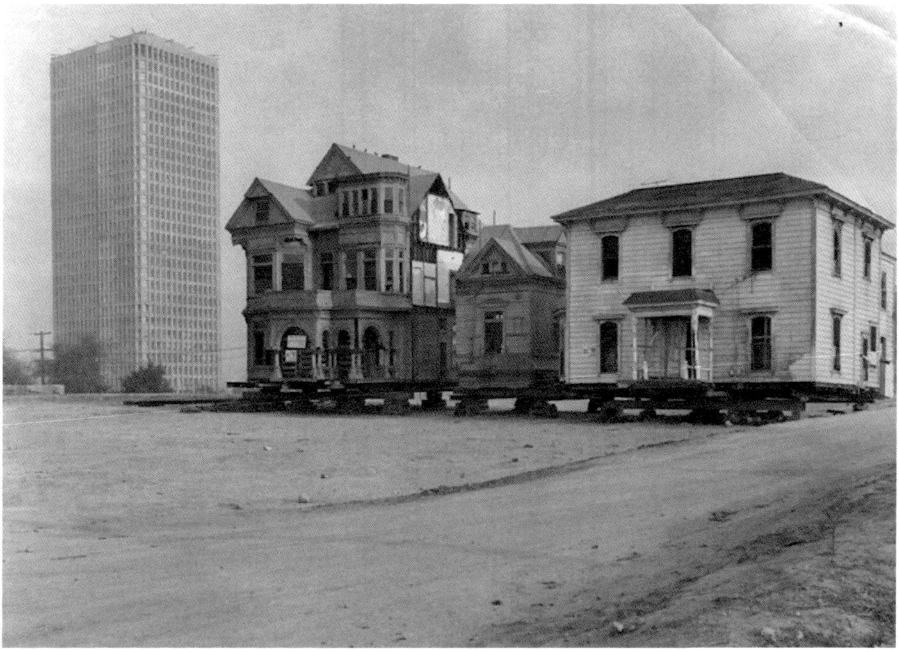

This photograph from 1969 shows two casualties from Los Angeles's Victorian past. Both "the Castle" (left) and the "Salt Box" (right) were destroyed in a fire shortly after being moved from Bunker Hill to the Heritage Square Museum in 1969. *Courtesy the Los Angeles Public Library.*

Completed in the late 1880s, the Palms Depot is a very rare surviving example of an Eastlake Victorian train station. Usage peaked between the 1920s and 1940s, when the station was used by many movie stars to get to nearby movie studios. After the Pacific Electric Red Cars ceased operations in 1953, however, the station was only used for occasional Boy Scout meetings and was threatened with demolition. Fortunately, activists groups succeeded in having the station moved to Heritage Square in 1976, where it currently serves as a gift shop and visitor's center.

For all of the success stories Heritage Square has had, there are, unfortunately, two buildings that were tragically lost. Two Bunker Hill homes—the "Salt Box," an incredibly unique example of "saltbox" architecture from the 1880s, and "the Castle," an 1882 Queen Anne mansion that sported twenty rooms, leaded glass doors and a hand-carved wooden stairway—were successfully moved to Heritage Square in 1969 as the site's first historic structures. A suspicious fire on October 9 of that same year, however, completely destroyed both homes.

Victorian Homes

Two other Victorian homes, while not part of a larger neighborhood, are so unique in their architecture that they deserve separate mentions.

EL ALISAL

When one thinks of a Victorian home, they typically think of the Queen Anne or Shingle styles that were so prevalent during the 1880s and 1890s. What one certainly does not think of is El Alisal, a home designed and built by Charles Fletcher Lummis around the turn of the twentieth century. One of Los Angeles's most interesting landmarks from the time, it represents an architectural style that is wholly innovative and unique.

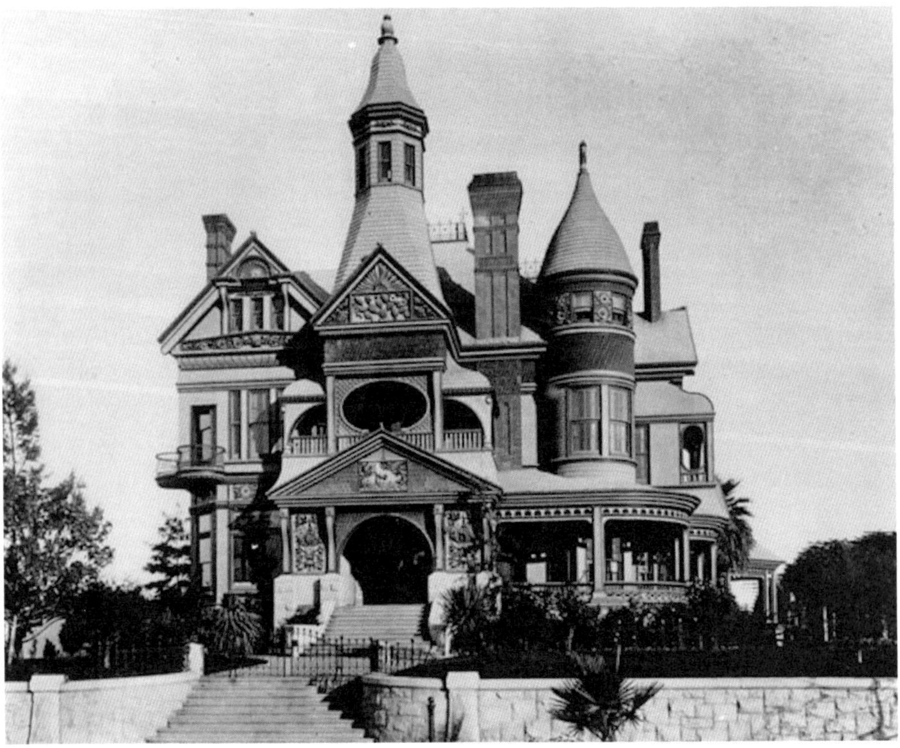

The Bradbury Mansion, located at Hill and Court Streets, was one of Los Angeles's most opulent Victorian homes. Owned by John Bradbury, whose father built the Bradbury Building, the mansion was used in a number of silent films before its demolition in 1929. *Courtesy the Los Angeles Public Library.*

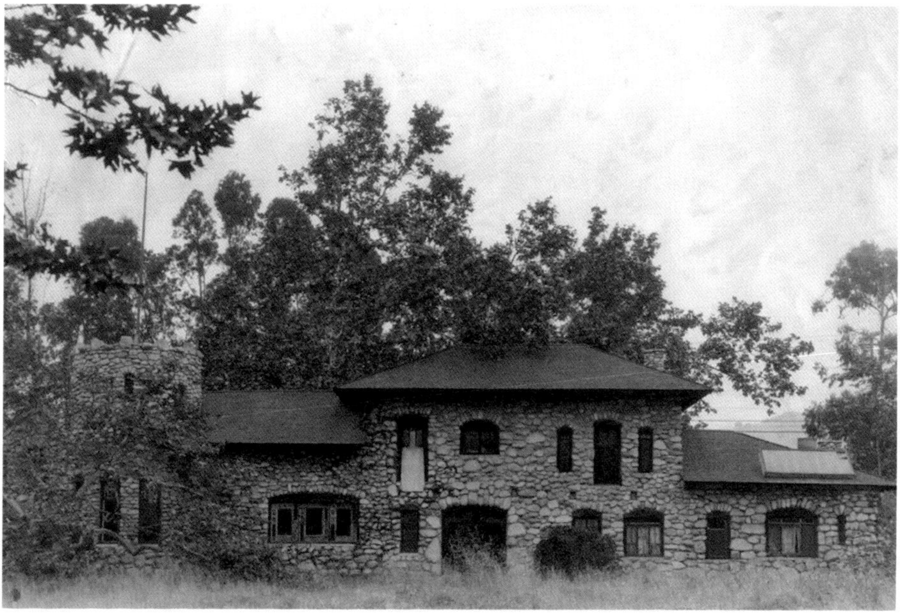

Perhaps the most unique Victorian-era home in Los Angeles, at least from an architectural standpoint, is Charles Fletcher Lummis's 1897 El Alisal ("the Alder Grove"). Lummis, the founder of the Southwest Museum, constructed the home's exterior using stones from the Arroyo Seco. *Courtesy the Los Angeles Public Library.*

Lummis, a Renaissance man of the Wild West, was a noted journalist, historian, photographer and Indian rights activist. When he decided to built his home on the Arroyo Seco northeast of Los Angeles, he incorporated elements of the missions and Native American dwellings he had seen during his frequent travels.

Built over a period of twelve years, there is nothing in Southern California quite like El Alisal. Constructed entirely from stones collected from the arroyo, Lummis's home has a rustic external look that is enhanced by exposed beams and handmade furniture inside. As the house was nearing completion, Lummis founded the Southwest Museum, an institution that is still active today.

Although threatened with demolition at various points in its history, El Alisal is currently protected as California State Historical Landmark #531 and is open to visitors on weekends (200 East Avenue 43).

STIMSON HOUSE

One of Los Angeles's most unique Victorian homes is the Stimson House, located just north of USC at 2421 Figueroa Street. Designed by Los Angeles architect H. Carroll Brown, the home was built in 1891 for Thomas Douglas

Stimson, who was a wealthy industrialist, businessman and vice-president of the Los Angeles Chamber of Commerce.

The Stimson House, which cost $130,000 to build, was by far the most expensive home in the city at the time. Sandstone was imported from New Mexico to furnish the outside of the thirty-room home, which features a four-story tower, brick chimneys and battlements along the rooftop (earning the building its nickname, "the Red Castle").

This home is by far the finest example of Richardson Romanesque architecture left in Los Angeles. Although the style was popular nationally in the 1890s, it never became prominent in Southern California. Many features, including the tower, also bear a strong resemblance to Victorian Gothic architecture. The interior is no less impressive than the exterior; each room on the lower floor was constructed with a different type of wood paneling, including mahogany, walnut and oak. The house also features stained-glass windows and a full basement, complete with a wine cellar.

A bizarre attack on the mansion took place in February 1896; an employee of Stimson, Harry Coyne, lit a stick of dynamite against the foundation of the house. Had the building been constructed of wood, it would have been destroyed completely, but the mansion's thick stone walls resisted the blast, and damage was minimal. Coyne was caught and sentenced to five years in Folsom Prison.

Over the years, the Stimson House also served as a fraternity house for USC students and dormitories for Mount St. Mary's College; today, it is a convent for the Sisters of St. Joseph. Although the home suffered considerable damage in the 1994 Northridge Earthquake, extensive reconstruction preserved the architectural integrity of the building. The house can still be seen from Figueroa, the last reminder of the opulent mansions that once lined the street.

Chapter 8

Traces of Victorian Los Angeles

Downtown

Although the face of downtown Los Angeles has been immeasurably changed during the twentieth century, there are still traces of he Victorian era if one knows where to look. Three buildings—the Pico House, St. Vibiana's and the Bradbury Building—stand out as the most significant Victorian landmarks, representing the final decades of the era. Because of their larger significance in the city's history, they are all described in detail elsewhere in this book. However, these are not the only Victorian landmarks one can encounter downtown; there are several other unsung architectural gems that also evoke this period of American history.

The Douglas Building (257 South Spring Street): Although not as spectacular as some of the Victorian buildings that once lined the streets of downtown, the Douglas Building is nonetheless a significant structure from the era. A five-story office building constructed right at the tail end of the Victorian period in 1898, the classically influenced architecture was the work of brothers James and Merritt Reid.

At its peak, the Douglas Building was among downtown's most prime real estate for corporate offices, with major tenants including the Southern Pacific Railroad. Although today the building's façade comes across as somewhat nondescript, at the time of its construction it marked a significant break from the oftentimes gaudy Victorian architecture that had been prevalent for so many years. In recent years, the Douglas Building (as is the case with many historic buildings downtown) has been converted into the Douglas Building Lofts.

The IRVINE-BYRNE BUILDING (249 South Broadway): Another rare example of a surviving office building from the 1890s, the Irvine-Byrne Building was one of the first projects designed by famed Los Angeles architect Sumner P. Hunt, who designed some of the region's most recognizable landmarks. When it opened in 1895, it faced Los Angeles's old city hall.

As with the Douglas Building, the Irvine-Byrne Block does not exhibit traditional Victorian architecture; instead, it draws from the Beaux-Arts style that was beginning to come into vogue at the turn of the century. Also present are subtle traces of the Spanish Colonial Revival style for which Hunt would become so well-known. After a $20 million renovation in 2004, the Irvine-Byrne Building is now home to the Pan American Lofts.

The VAN NUYS (BARCLAY) HOTEL (103 West Fourth Street): Designed by Octavius Morgan and J.A. Walls and constructed between 1895 and 1896, the Van Nuys Hotel was one of the first "modern" hotels to be constructed in downtown Los Angeles. The Beaux-Arts style is again indicative of the new wave of construction beginning in the last years of the nineteenth century, when Victorian-style architecture was beginning to fade into the past.

Renamed the Barclay Hotel in 1929, the building has undergone substantial renovation over the years and has been the victim of several arson fires. Today, the building serves as a low-income hotel and boardinghouse. It has the distinction of being Los Angeles's oldest continuously operating hotel.

The HOMER LAUGHLIN BUILDING (317 South Broadway): Although known today as Grand Central Market, the Homer Laughlin Building was constructed by the retired founder of the china company with that same name. The building was designed by John Parkinson, who would go on to design some of the city's most important landmarks.

Originally, the Homer Laughlin Building was occupied by the Ville de Paris Department Store, but in 1917, the ground floor became Grand Central Market—still a staple of downtown Los Angeles today. The nearby Angels Flight provided easy access to the market for residents living on Bunker Hill. Although not the most impressive of Los Angeles's Victorian office buildings downtown, the Homer Laughlin Building nonetheless is a significant part of the city's history.

The RAPHAEL JUNCTION BLOCK BUILDING (1635 North Spring Street): A unique example of flatiron architecture and one of the last remaining vestiges of Los Angeles's North Industrial District neighborhood, the Raphael Junction Block Building was constructed in 1889. Over the years, it has served as the home of the California Ice Company, the New York

Suspender Factory and the Raphael Glass Company (for whose founder, Charles Raphael, the building is named).

Once a prosperous train yard and industrial area, the area surrounding the Raphael Junction Building is now all but forgotten. The adjacent Los Angeles State Historic Park has conducted numerous archaeological excavations to uncover the neighborhood's unique role in shaping the early history of Los Angeles. UCLA currently runs its Interpretive Media Laboratory out of the building, helping to create public awareness about the park.

VICTORIAN TRAIN STATIONS

Today, Los Angeles has only one major train depot—the late 1930s Union Station located just north of downtown. However, few people today realize that prior to this, each railroad that ran trains in and out of Los Angeles had its own depot specifically for its own use. At one time, the Union Pacific, Southern Pacific, Santa Fe and other smaller railroads all had their own stations, several of which were among Los Angeles's lost Victorian jewels.

The first Los Angeles train depot notable for its architecture was that of the Los Angeles & Independence Railroad, which connected downtown to Santa Monica in 1875. The station, located on San Pedro Street between Fourth and Fifth Streets (across from Winston Street), featured lavish and eclectic architecture that invoked both the Italianate and French Second Empire styles. This early in the city's history, such ornate buildings were not the norm, making the depot stand out considerably.

Due to the short lifespan of the LA&I Railroad, the building stopped serving as a passenger terminal after only five years; between 1880 and the fire that ultimately destroyed the building in 1888, the former depot was used as storage for various industries.

The two stations that epitomize the Victorian era in Los Angeles were undoubtedly the Southern Pacific's Arcade Depot and the Santa Fe's La Grande Depot. Both showcased radically different architectural styles but demonstrated the prominent role that Los Angeles was beginning to play in the western United States at this time.

The older of the two, the Arcade Depot, was built in 1888 and opened the following year. Constructed of wood supported by iron trusses, the station was monumental in size. Five hundred feet long, eighty feet wide and sporting a ninety-foot-tall arched roof, the Arcade Depot epitomized the

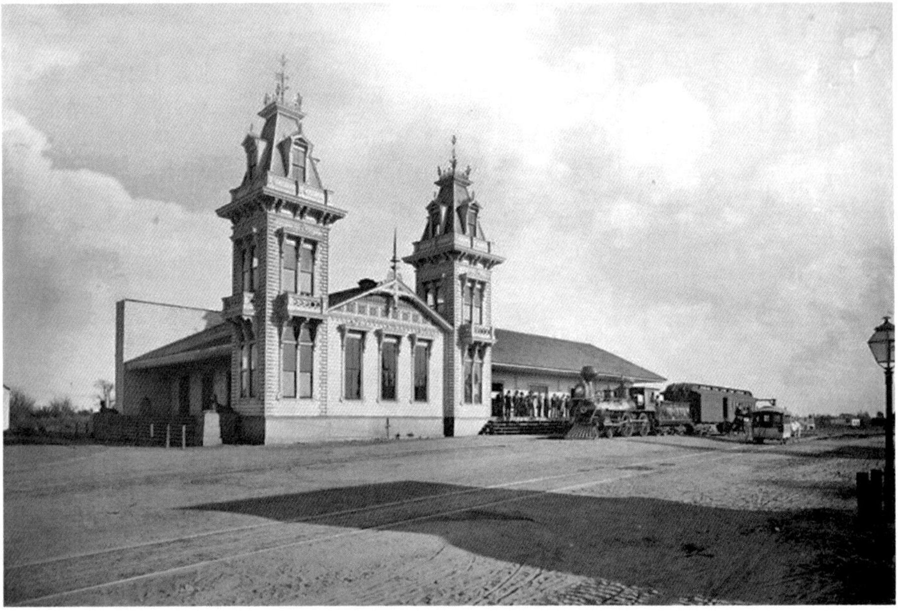

A circa 1875 view of the Los Angeles & Independence Railroad depot on San Pedro Street. The ornate Victorian building would only serve as a train station for five years; from 1880 to 1888, it was used as storage before ultimately burning to the ground. *Courtesy Water and Power Associates.*

Romanesque style that was peaking in popularity during the late 1880s. Its vaulted roof had skylights to naturally illuminate the inside of the station, and the building's four corners were marked with impressive turrets.

Replaced after only twenty-five years in 1914, the Arcade Depot could only have been a product of the Victorian period, and images of it evoke the great train stations of Europe from this same time. Changes in technology, as well as shifting cultural norms, spelled the station's demise. Its former location, near the intersection of Alameda and Fifth Streets, is now occupied by warehouses.

One remnant of the Arcade Station lives on to this day—quite literally. In front of the Los Angeles Coliseum in Exposition Park sits a palm tree that some claim is the oldest tree in Los Angeles. Probably born in the 1850s, the palm was transported to the entrance of the Southern Pacific Railroad's Arcade Station downtown, welcoming visitors to Los Angeles from across the country. This is where it remained until the station's demolition in 1914, at which time preservationists succeeded in moving the tree to Exposition Park, where it has thrived ever since.

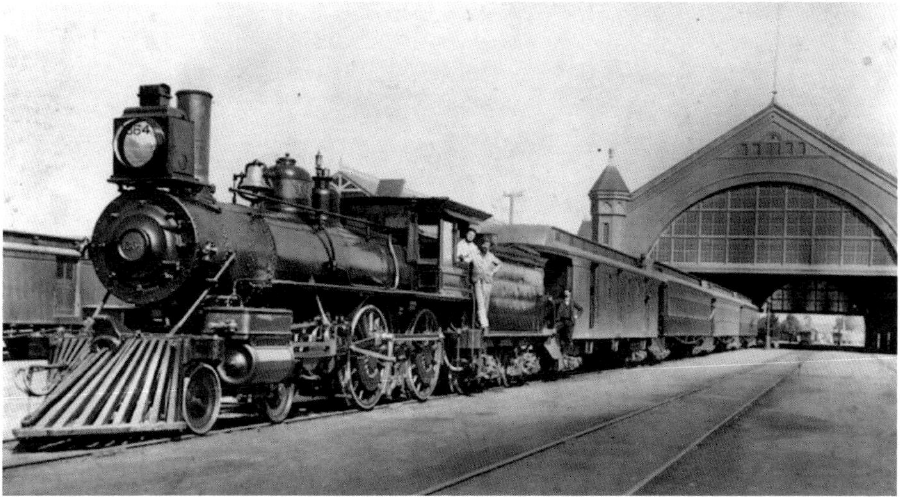

A train is seen outside the Southern Pacific Arcade Depot in this 1891 photograph. Prior to the construction of Union Station in 1939, each railroad that ran into Los Angeles had its own individual passenger depot. This building was demolished in 1914. *Courtesy the Los Angeles Public Library.*

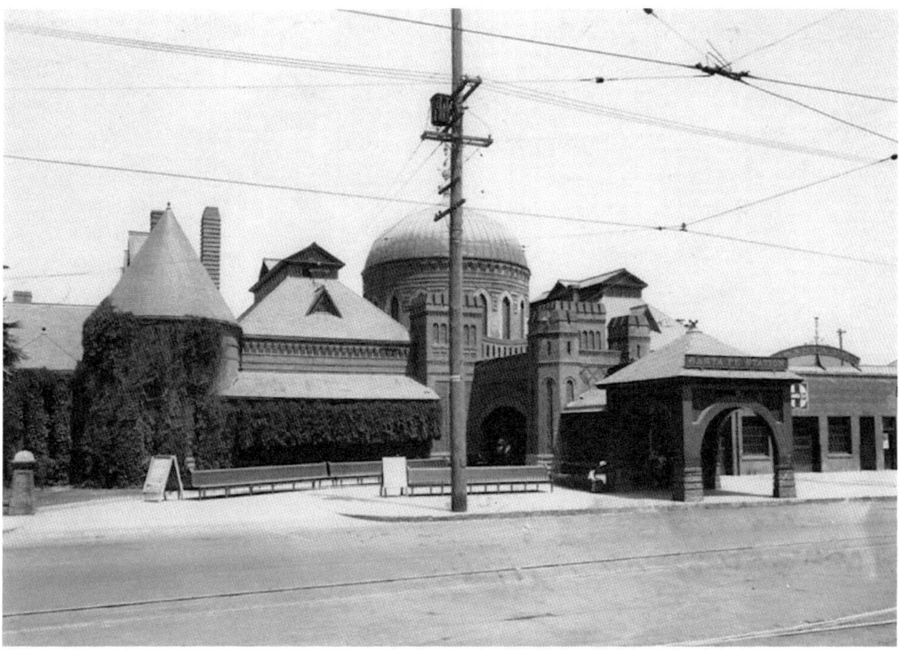

One of the most unique buildings in Los Angeles's long history, the Atchison, Topeka & Santa Fe Railway's La Grande Station opened in 1893. Its eclectic architecture was a mixture of Moorish, Richardsonian Romanesque and Mission styles. *Courtesy the Los Angeles Public Library.*

The last of Los Angeles's Victorian train depots that will be covered here is the Atchison, Topeka & Santa Fe Railway's La Grande Station, opened in 1893 at Second Street and Santa Fe Avenue. Whereas the Arcade Depot conformed to Victorian architectural norms, the La Grande Depot was unlike anything the city had ever seen before.

The station's most prominent influence, as seen in its large central onion dome, is Moorish architecture. Another factor that set the La Grande Station apart from its contemporaries was the fact that it was constructed from brick, as opposed to the wooden stations of the past. While visually appealing, this construction tactic also made the station vulnerable to earthquakes (as would be the case in 1933, when the large dome was removed due to irreparable damage).

One researcher also characterized the building's design as the "transition between Richardsonian Romanesque and Mission style" architecture—the outdated Romanesque being replaced by the Mission Revival movement that would come to embody Southern California.

Because of the stunning nature of the station, it became a popular filming location during the first decades of the twentieth century, and it managed to hang on until Union Station opened to passengers in 1939.

Today, no real trace remains of any of Los Angeles's Victorian train stations, which showcased a wide range of architectural styles locally popular during the time. As impressive as Union Station's "Spanish Colonial meets Art Deco" design is, it is important to remember the rail history of Los Angeles as well, as it was one of the key factors in shaping the city into a major metropolis.

STREETS

One of the most important remnants of Los Angeles's Victorian days are the very streets that crisscross downtown to this day. The story of these streets also ties into one of the most significant artifacts in the city's history: a map drawn by an army lieutenant in 1849.

It was in 1849 that Lieutenant Edward Ord, who would later play a significant role in the Civil War, was hired to conduct a survey of Los Angeles for official city business. Along with his assistant, William Rich Hutton, Ord spent the months of July and August conducting the first full-scale survey of the city, and he eventually produced the first accurate map of the Plaza and its surrounding neighborhoods.

Dated August 29, 1849, Ord and Hutton's map provides an incredible wealth of information regarding what the city was like on the eve of California's statehood. When compared with Los Angeles today, the city appears minuscule; no development is shown south of Eighth Street, and all that occupies the east bank of the Los Angeles River is farmland. The region's natural topography dominates much of the map, with the city proper only extending short distances north and south of the Plaza.

What stands out to someone looking at the map today are the unfamiliar street names. With the exception of downtown's numbered east–west streets, many of the names used on Ord's map have been changed in the century and a half since it was first published.

Among the north–south streets located to the south of the Plaza, some were simply translated from Spanish, while others were actually changed. Main Street, for example, was simply changed from Calle Principal over time. Likewise, Calle Primavera became Spring Street, Calle Loma became Hill Street, Calle Accytuna (*Aceituna*) became Olive Street, Calle de Las Esperanzas became Hope Street and Calle de Las Flores became Flower Street.

Of the names that were changed, several have interesting stories behind them. Broadway, for instance, was originally Calle Fortin (Fort Street) because it terminated at Fort Moore Hill to the north. It wouldn't be until 1890 that Fort Moore was far enough in the past for the name to be changed.

Grand Avenue was known as Calle de Caridad (Charity Street) until 1887. Along with Hope Street and Flower Street (supposedly a stand in for "faith"), these three streets represented the three theological virtues in the Christian tradition. However, legend has it that enough people complained about having to "live on Charity" for the name to be changed.

Figueroa Street, the westernmost street shown on Ord's map, was originally called Calle de Los Chapules, or Grasshopper Street, because of the massive swarms of grasshoppers that lived in the fields west of the city. In the 1880s, it became known as Pearl Street but was eventually renamed after Mexican governor José Figueroa.

North of the Plaza, in modern-day Chinatown, almost no street names on the map are recognizable today. Running north–south, Spring Street was originally known as Calle Principal (Main Street), while Broadway was originally called Calle de Eternidad (Eternity Street) because "it had neither beginning nor end, or, rather, each end terminated in the hills."

Hill Street was known as Calle del Toro (Bull Street) because it was home to the city's bullfighting arena, while Calle de Las Avispas (Hornet Street, now Yale Street) was a reference to the area's frequent infestations of wasps.

Adobe Street, of which a small portion still remains, retained its original name of Calle de Los Adobes.

Chinatown's east–west streets have likewise undergone significant changes—Calle Corta (Short Street) approximately became Cesar Chavez Avenue, Calle Alta (High Street) became Ord Street (after the map's creator) and Calle de Las Virgines (Virgin Street) became Alpine Street. Calle de Colegio is still known as College Street.

Although little more than historical footnotes now, these long-forgotten street names nevertheless give insight into the Los Angeles during the second half of the nineteenth century and provide some amusing stories about the city's formation. Street layouts and names are often taken for granted, but it is important to remember their circumstances of their origins.

Chapter 9

Traces of Victorian Los Angeles

Historic Parks

Los Angeles is fortunate to have several designated historic parks that focus on the city's Victorian history. While all vastly different in their temporal, geographical and historical scope, they are all important contributions to the preservation and study of the development of the city during the nineteenth century.

Los Angeles State Historic Park

Founded in 2001, Los Angeles State Historic Park is a thirty-two-acre plot of land located north of downtown, adjacent to Chinatown and Elysian Park. The mission of the park is to chronicle Los Angeles's history dating back thousands of years, from the time of the Tongva Indians all the way through the modern period. For the purposes of this book, the park's focus on the Southern Pacific Railroad is most significant.

In 1875, the Southern Pacific Railroad opened the River Station on the site that is now the State Historic Park. Known as the "Ellis Island of Los Angeles," this station welcomed countless passengers to Los Angeles and served as the southern end of the transcontinental railroad. Within a few years, the rail yard had become home to a roundhouse, a turntable, a depot, a hotel and other amenities for both people and products arriving in the city.

With the River Station as its hub, the surrounding area quickly developed into an important industrial district; at the time, Los Angeles's population had not yet begun to shift toward the south. However, by the late 1880s, the River Station had become outdated and impractical and was swiftly replaced by a larger station nearer to the city's metropolitan center.

For many years, the site of the River Station was known as "the Cornfield," as kernels of corn would fall off incoming freight trains and sprout up along the tracks. In 1992, Southern Pacific sold the Cornfield to the State of California, and work on turning it into an accessible historic site began in early 2014. The completed park is set to open to the public in the summer of 2015.

When finished, the park will showcase the sites of the Pacific Hotel, River Station Depot, Roundhouse, Maintenance Yard and other features of the former River Station Area. Also included will be a recently uncovered segment of the Zanja Madre (Los Angeles's first irrigation system), the park's Native American history and walking trails to all of the aforementioned landmarks.

SANTA SUSANA PASS STATE HISTORIC PARK

Located between Chatsworth and Simi Valley, Santa Susana Pass State Historic Park preserves a segment of the stagecoach trail that once connected Los Angeles with Ventura County and, further on, San Francisco. Before the railroad connected Northern and Southern California in 1876, this route was invaluable in transporting travelers, products and mail.

The first overland crossing of the Santa Susana Pass came on April 6, 1861, and this trail quickly surpassed the former route through the Tejon Pass as the main artery between San Francisco and Los Angeles. Although serving as a prominent stagecoach trail for only fifteen years, the Santa Susana Stage Road played an integral role in California's history at the critical transition between the stagecoach era and the railroad era.

The most dangerous section of the road was known as the Devil's Slide; visitors to the area today, which was at one time so treacherous that horses needed to be blindfolded in order for them to proceed, can still see stagecoach ruts in the ground from the countless trips made through the pass. The Native Daughters of the Golden West placed a mosaic plaque at the site in 1939, commemorating the route's importance to regional history.

PIO PICO STATE HISTORIC PARK

Pio Pico State Historic Park preserves El Ranchito, the final home of famed Californian Pio Pico. Pico served as the last Mexican governor of Alta California, and following the acceptance of California into the Union, he continued to live in the Los Angeles area as an American citizen. He began acquiring the land around the site—present-day Whittier—in the 1840s, immediately following the conclusion of the Mexican-American War; he built his house on the property, which he named El Ranchito (the little ranch) in about 1853.

Despite acquiring a sizable fortune, Pico was the victim of numerous bad circumstances and died almost broke at the house of his daughter in 1894. Almost immediately upon his death, the importance of El Ranchito was recognized, and for nearly a century, the home has been owned and protected by the State of California.

As the home of one of the most prominent residents of Los Angeles during the Victorian era, Pio Pico State Historic Park serves as a reminder of how Mexican culture persisted and merged with American culture at the time of California's separation from Mexico. Although not "Victorian" by traditional standards, El Ranchito still serves as a means to learn what life was like in late nineteenth-century Los Angeles (a city that never truly conformed to Victorian culture).

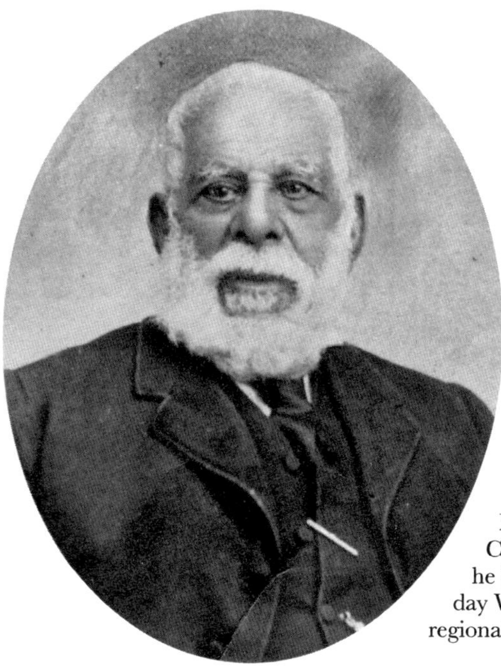

Few men did more to shape the history of California than Pio Pico, who served as the last Mexican governor of the state before the Mexican-American War. Following California's admittance into the Union, he lived out the rest of his life in present-day Whittier and remained a prominent regional figure. *Courtesy the Whittier Museum.*

Los Encinos State Historic Park

Los Encinos State Historic Park, located in the modern community of Encino, contains buildings that showcase different eras of Los Angeles's history. The oldest building on the property is the De la Ossa Adobe, which dates back to 1850 (making it one of the oldest adobe structures in the county).

After changing ownership, a two-story limestone building was constructed on the property in the 1870s, as was a pond that is still fed to this day by a natural spring. Both of these features are still present as part of the state park and show how many of the ranchos in the area developed over the decades after they passed into the hands of Americans. While by no means the only adobe preserved in Los Angeles County, Los Encinos State Historic Park provides visitors with a sense of what life would have been like on a typical nineteenth-century rancho.

Los Angeles Plaza Historic District

The Los Angeles Plaza is arguably the most historic location within the entire city, dating back to its very founding in 1781. For much of Los Angeles's history, the Plaza was the center of civic government, social life and commerce. And since the creation of Olvera Street in 1930, its status as a tourist destination has been planted firmly in the Spanish and Mexican eras of the city's history.

Despite being home to early landmarks such as the Avila Adobe (Los Angeles's oldest home, dating to 1818), the Plaza also contains a number of structures dating to the height of the Victorian era, between 1870 and the turn of the twentieth century. Partly due to the Plaza's long-standing historic status, these buildings were preserved at a much higher rate than elsewhere in the city and serve as a kind of living history museum showcasing Los Angeles in the nineteenth century.

Vickrey-Brunswig Building (501 North Main Street)

Located on the west side of North Main Street, the Vickrey-Brunswig Building was one of Los Angeles's first five-story buildings when it opened in 1888. Its Italianate architecture—complementing other nearby buildings from this era—was designed by Robert Brown Young, one of Los Angeles's prominent architects during the 1880s. It was commissioned by William Vickrey, a businessman, for use as retail space on the ground floor and housing on the four upper floors.

During the early years of the twentieth century, the building was home to the Brunswig Drug Company; from the 1940s onward, it was used by the county as offices for various departments. Between the mid-1970s and the 2000s, the building sat vacant and quickly fell into a state of disrepair.

In 2011, following an extensive renovation, the Vickrey-Brunswig Building was reopened to the public as the LA Plaza de Cultura y Artes, a cultural center dedicated to the Mexican-American experience in Los Angeles. As part of this project, the building's façade was restored to its original appearance, making it an integral part of Los Angeles's Victorian history.

Plaza House (507 North Main Street)

The Plaza House was designed in 1883 by the noted firm of Ezra Kysor and Octavius Morgan, which had a hand in designing many of the city's early landmarks. Also known as the Garnier Block (not to be confused with the nearby Garnier Building, built by the same French immigrant), the Plaza House shares much of its recent history with the Vickrey-Brunswig Building.

After originally serving as a hotel and retail building, the Plaza House was converted into county offices during the 1940s alongside the Vickrey-Brunswig Building. Beginning in the 1970s, these two buildings sat vacant for three decades; however, in their renovation during the 2000s, both buildings were connected internally and jointly serve as the home of the LA Plaza de Cultura y Artes today.

Merced Theatre (420 North Main Street)

Located next to the Pico House is Los Angeles's first theater, the Merced. Its Italianate design matches that of the Pico House (thanks to their shared architect, Ezra Kysor) and harkens back to a style that was only popular in Los Angeles for a brief period during the 1870s.

The theater was built by William Abbot and named after his wife, Maria Merced Garcia. For the first several years of its existence, the Merced Theatre was the center of the city's social life. However, as the city expanded and the nearby Wood's Opera House opened, the Merced gained an unsavory reputation as the quality of entertainment declined sharply. It closed on New Year's Day 1877.

After sitting vacant for many years, the Merced Theatre was recently converted into office space for a local news television station, ensuring that Los Angeles's first theater will continue to stand for many years to come.

Masonic Hall (416 North Main Street)

Completing the Pico House–Merced Theatre block, the Masonic Hall was constructed in 1858—making it not only the oldest building of these three but also the oldest building in Los Angeles south of the Plaza. It is an early example of Italianate architecture, which would be further developed and expanded on for its neighbors.

Los Angeles Masonic Lodge No. 42, founded in 1853, was the first American organization founded in Los Angeles and is the second-oldest lodge in Southern California. It occupied the upper floor of this hall for only a decade before moving elsewhere in 1868. Meanwhile, the ground floor was used by a carpentry shop that specialized in making coffins.

After serving a number of purposes over the years, the 1858 Masonic Lodge was reoccupied by the Masons in 1981, almost 130 years after the order was originally founded in Los Angeles. It still serves this purpose today, in addition to being part of the El Pueblo Historic Monument.

Garnier Building (423 North Los Angeles Street)

Located behind the Merced Theatre on Los Angeles Street, the Garnier Building is one of a small handful of surviving commercial buildings from the Victorian era. Built in 1890—as marked on the building's pediment—the Garnier Building originally housed shops on its ground floor and community space on the second floor.

Although built by a French immigrant, Phillipe Garnier, the Garnier Building is perhaps most notable for being the oldest surviving Chinese building in Southern California, as well as the only building remaining from Los Angeles's original Chinatown. The second floor was used as a Chinese school, a temple and a meeting hall at a time when anti-Chinese sentiment in the city was rampant.

In the late 1940s, the Garnier Block fell into the hands of the city; it was a few years after this that the southern third of the building was demolished to make way for the 101 Freeway. In December 2003, the building opened its doors once again, this time as the Chinese American Museum—a fitting location for an institution dedicated to preserving the history of Chinese culture in Los Angeles.

Plaza Firehouse (501 North Los Angeles Street)

Although Los Angeles has had a volunteer fire department since the early 1870s, the city's oldest firehouse—located on the plaza—would not be constructed until 1884. A brick building featuring a restored wooden cupola and balcony, the Plaza Firehouse has, since 1960, served as a museum dedicated to preserving the history of firefighting in the city.

William Boring, the architect for the firehouse, modeled his plans off of fire stations in his native state of Illinois. A unique turntable in the center made it easier to get the horse-drawn engines in and out of the building. Within a year and a half of its completion in August 1884, Los Angeles established its first paid fire department—in large part due to the new facilities.

The building's tenure as a firehouse was relatively short-lived, as in 1897 the department moved its operations to a building more suited for the growing city. The Plaza Firehouse went on to serve as a saloon, a hotel and various stores and markets before preservationists stepped in to convert it to its current state.

Sepulveda House (622 North Main Street)

The Sepulveda House is a twenty-two-room Eastlake Victorian–style house that was constructed in 1887. When it was originally built by Señora Eloisa Martiniez de Sepulveda, the front rooms of the mixed-use building served as shops, while the back and upper floor were used for lodging.

The building's unique architecture, which highlights the transition from Mexican to American culture in Los Angeles, was designed by George F. Costerisan and William O. Merithew, one of Los Angeles's early architectural duos. Señora Sepulveda lived in the house's back units until her death in 1903; although she deeded the building to her niece, it soon fell into disrepair.

In the 1930s, a woman by the name of Christine Sterling almost single-handedly crafted Olvera Street into the tourist destination it is today. Part of her revitalization plan included the Sepulveda House, which went on to house the famous "Yale Puppeteers" and a USO Canteen over the years. Today, the building serves as a visitor center and museum for the El Pueblo de Los Angeles Historical Monument.

Chapter 10

A Brief Tour of Downtown Victorian Los Angeles

To help paint a better picture of what Los Angeles was actually like during the Victorian era, this final section is a guided tour of three of downtown's most prominent thoroughfares around the turn of the twentieth century. Very few of the buildings described still exist today, so while walking downtown, it is haunting to think of how radically different the city once was.

The three roads covered—Broadway, Spring Street and Main Street—were chosen because of the high concentration of buildings constructed during the late Victorian era and demolished at various times during the twentieth century. These tours are by no means comprehensive, as a complete guide to every building downtown is beyond the scope of this book. Instead, it is merely representative of what someone in 1900 might have seen during the course of a normal day.

Broadway

Standing at the intersection of Temple Street and Broadway, you would have immediately been faced with an incredibly imposing structure: the fortress-like County Courthouse, which opened in 1891. With its striking Romanesque architecture and impenetrable red sandstone walls, the courthouse was unlike anything the city of Los Angeles had seen before. Perched on Poundcake Hill, its clock tower could be seen for miles.

Catty-corner the courthouse, on the northwest side of the intersection, was the Temperance Temple of the Women's Christian Temperance Union, whose Southern California chapter was founded in 1883. Its four-story stone headquarters was built in 1889 after a generous donation to the organization several years earlier. Later on, the top story of the building featured a school for girls.

Walking south, crossing First Street and approaching Second, there was an eclectic mix of architectural styles. On the near right-hand side was the Frost Building, designed by an up-and-coming architect named John Parkinson in 1898. Parkinson and his son, Donald, would go on to design some of Los Angeles's most recognizable landmarks like city hall and the Memorial Coliseum.

Across Second Street was the California Bank Building, a textbook Queen Anne–style building from 1887. Also known as the American National Bank Building, this structure featured hallmarks of the Victorian era such as a corner turret and ornate brickwork. Next to

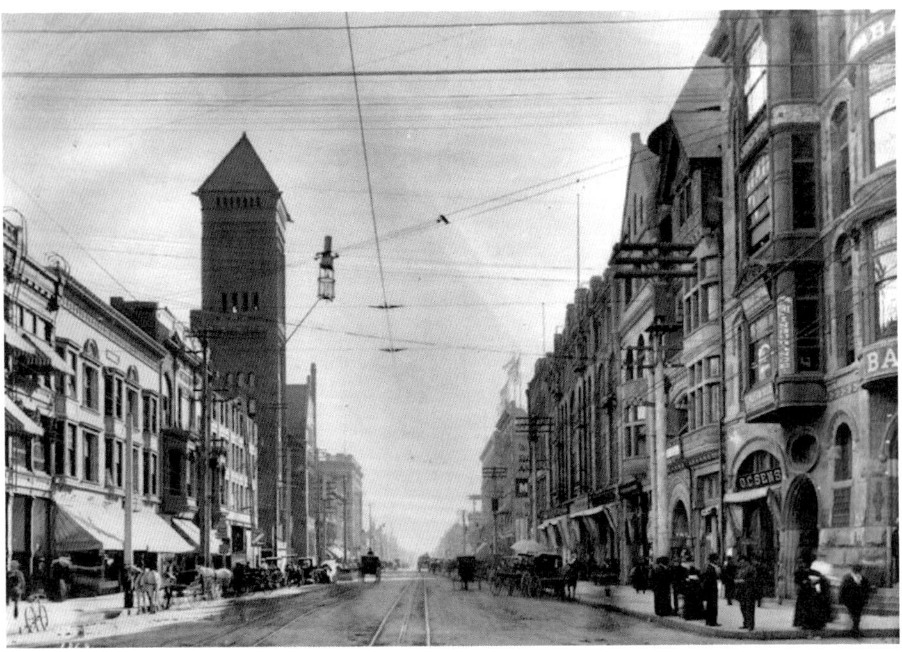

Broadway looking south from Second Street in 1895. The large tower seen on the left is Los Angeles's Romanesque city hall. Within the first decades of the twentieth century, street scenes such as this would be changed dramatically by redevelopment. *Courtesy the Los Angeles Public Library.*

the California Bank Building was the city's first YMCA building, which featured impressive Victorian architecture in its own right.

Almost directly across from the YMCA building was city hall. When it first opened in 1888, city hall stood almost by itself on the block, but over the years, other buildings closed in on either side of it until little more than the façade was visible.

Continuing past city hall to Third Street are two of downtown's only Victorian buildings that are still standing today. The northwest corner features the Irvine-Byrne Building, designed by Sumner P. Hunt, while the southeast corner is home to the Bradbury Building, arguably Los Angeles's most celebrated Victorian landmark. Although neither is particularly remarkable from the outside, they are nonetheless important parts in preserving this time in the city's history. Only a block farther south from the Bradbury Building was the Mason Building, constructed between 1893 and 1894. The Los Angeles Chamber of Commerce called the Mason Building home for nine years until 1903.

Today, with the exception of the Irvine-Byrne Block (now the Pan American Lofts) and the Bradbury Building, Broadway has been entirely transformed. Once home to most of the city's civic infrastructure, Broadway quickly became known for its historic theaters during the twentieth century. For a number of reasons, ranging from safety concerns to changing architectural tastes, nearly the entire street was transformed over the course of just several decades.

Spring Street

One block to the east of Broadway is Spring Street, another of the major north–south arteries through downtown. In about 1900, it was home to many of the city's most prominent hotels and businesses. Standing at the intersection of Temple Street looking south, the old Romanesque County Courthouse would this time be on the right, while on the left, midway down the block, would be the Bullard Block. Inspired by the French Second Empire style of architecture, this five-story office building sat on the current site of Los Angeles's city hall.

At the intersection of Spring and First Streets was the Larronde Block, the Wilson Block and the Hotel Nadeau. The Larronde Block, on the northwest corner, was built in 1882 by a prominent sheep rancher and

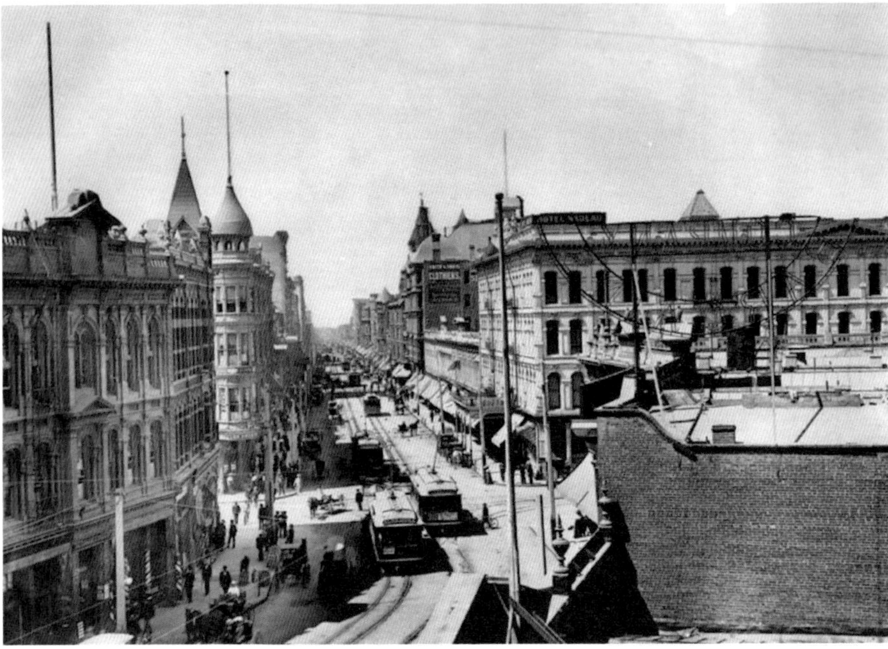

This 1880 photograph was taken looking south on Spring Street from First Street. The ornate tower seen on the far left corner is the Hotel Nadeau, Los Angeles's first four-story building. *Courtesy the Los Angeles Public Library.*

gold miner. Its appearance was very similar to the Pico House, showing a strong influence of the Italianate style of architecture.

Across First Street to the south was the Hotel Nadeau, Los Angeles's first four-story building. A commanding building topped with classical pediments, the Nadeau stood from 1885 until 1932; for much of its early history, it was one of the city's finest hotels. Shortly after its demolition, the Los Angeles Times Building was constructed on the same corner.

Across from the Hotel Nadeau and catty-corner to the Larronde Block was the Wilson Block, constructed in 1886 by a Mrs. C. Wilson. The Wilson Block was best known for featuring one of Los Angeles's multiple distinctive cupolas, which used to be prominent features of the city's skyline.

Two more buildings with cupolas—the Bryson-Bonebrake Block and the Hollenbeck Hotel—occupied the intersection one block south, at Second Street. The Bryson Block, on the northwest corner, stood six stories high and cost nearly $250,000 when it was built in 1888. Unceremoniously demolished around the same time as the Hotel Nadeau, it was at one time touted as one of Los Angeles's most elegant office buildings.

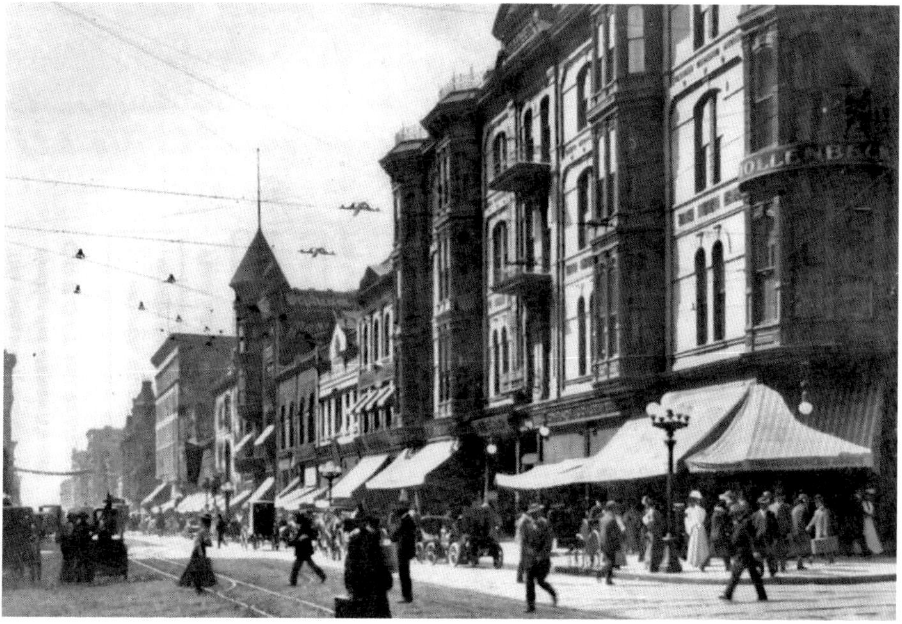

This circa 1898 view of Spring Street shows the Hollenbeck Hotel in the foreground. Built in 1884 and demolished in 1931, the ornate hotel featured a five-story octagonal tower. The only building still standing in this photo is the Douglass Building, which can be seen in the distance. *Courtesy the Los Angeles Public Library.*

A more traditionally Victorian-styled building, the Hollenbeck Hotel, was located across Second Street to the south. Built in 1884 by John Hollenbeck, one of Los Angeles's most prominent businessmen at the time, it was considered to be one of the city's finest hotels alongside the nearby Nadeau and Westminster.

Continuing down the 200 block of Spring Street were the Los Angeles Theater and the Douglas Block, the latter of which is still standing today at the intersection of Spring and Third Streets. Also at this intersection were the Ramona Hotel, the Stimson Building (Los Angeles's first six-story building) and the Lankershim Building (outdoing the Stimson Block by becoming the city's first seven-story building). None of these three structures managed to survive the first several decades of the twentieth century, leaving almost no trace of Los Angeles's Victorian past on this stretch of Spring Street.

MAIN STREET

One of Los Angeles's oldest streets, Main Street serves as the divider between east and west addresses for downtown's numbered streets. It was also home to many of the city's most prominent landmarks during the Victorian era. The 100 block of North Main Street alone was home to both the Amestoy Building and the U.S. Hotel, both of which featured typical Victorian commercial architecture typical of the 1880s and '90s. The Amestoy Building vied with the Hotel Nadeau for laying claim to Los Angeles's first elevator sometime during the 1880s.

Across the street from the U.S. Hotel was the St. Elmo Hotel, constructed during the 1850s as the LaFayette Hotel. Also known as the Cosmopolitan Hotel for a short while, the St. Elmo was at one time considered Los Angeles's finest hotel. Also on the same block, near the present site of city hall, was the Temple Block, owned by prominent local Jonathan Temple (for whom the street is also named).

Located on the southeast corner of Main and First Streets, where CalTrans is currently located, was once the Grand Opera House (also known as Child's Opera House). Home to many pivotal events in the early history of Los Angeles from the time it opened in 1884, it was here that Sarah Bernhardt ("the most famous actress the world has ever known") performed her signature role in *La Tosca* on September 14, 1891. It was also at the Grand Opera House that the city's first exhibition of motion pictures took place in 1896, a critical event for a place that would soon become synonymous with the cinematic arts.

Continuing down Main Street, St. Vibiana's Cathedral (discussed earlier in this book) is located one block south of where the opera house would have been. Several blocks farther south were two of Los Angeles's most fashionable hotels—one of which is still standing, while the other is not. The Van Nuys Hotel, on the northwest corner of Main and Fourth Streets, was opened in 1896 and is still in operation as the Barclay Hotel.

Located across Main Street to the east was the Westminster Hotel, undoubtedly one of the most architecturally striking buildings in the city's history. Robert B. Young was the architect for the 1887 building, which showed a strong influence of the Queen Anne style and featured a landmark six-story tower. The Westminster managed to hold on longer than many other buildings downtown but eventually succumbed to redevelopment in February 1960.

Half a block south of the Westminster Hotel, the United States government constructed a Federal Building on the corner of Main and

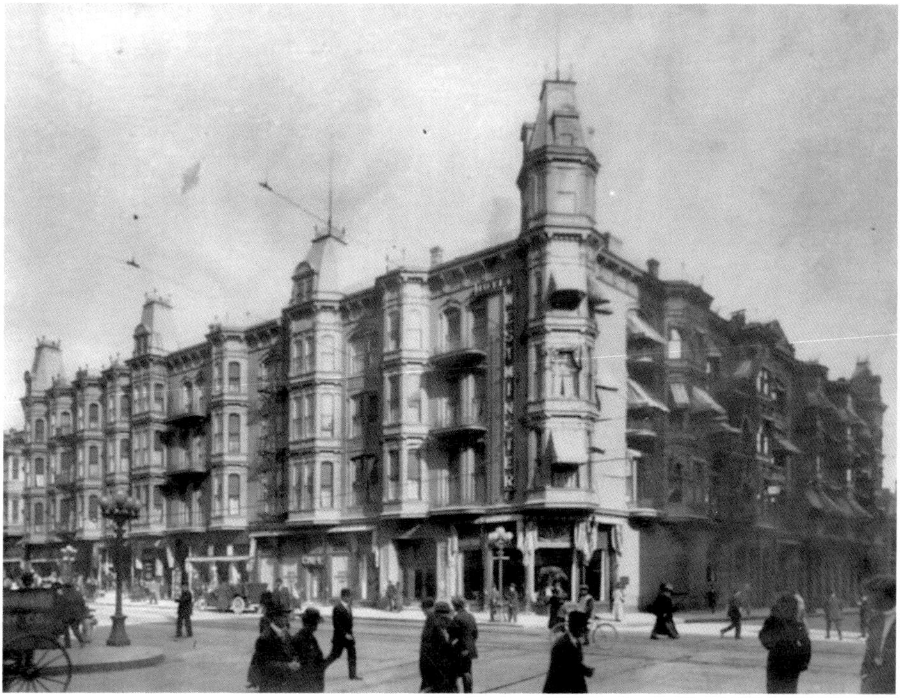

Once considered the finest hotel in Los Angeles, and epitomizing typical metropolitan Victorian architecture, the Westminster Hotel was built in 1887 at the corner of Fourth and Main Streets. The ornate structure was demolished in 1960; today, the corner is home to an apartment building. *Courtesy the Los Angeles Public Library.*

Winston Streets. Opened in 1893, the turreted Romanesque building housed the city's post office (among other federal offices) for a short while until a new structure was completed in 1908.

All three of the streets described—Broadway, Spring and Main—have undergone substantial change since the turn of the twentieth century, and these brief tours are simply meant as a way to demonstrate the extent that downtown has changed. While similar pieces could be written about other streets in the vicinity, none match the sheer number of Victorian landmarks on these three.

EPILOGUE

THE END OF VICTORIAN LOS ANGELES

On the evening of January 22, 1901, Queen Victoria passed away. News of her death filled the front page of the *Los Angeles Times* for several days but was quickly replaced by more pressing local stories. Although many British immigrants gathered at the YMCA to mourn her death, the news had little immediate effect on the city. The Victorian era of England had come to a close, and life in Los Angeles—as would be expected—carried on as usual.

The end of the Victorian era in Los Angeles did not coincide with the death of Queen Victoria; instead, as mentioned in the introduction and throughout this text, the close of the Victorian era came as a result of several unrelated changes that occurred in the city around this time.

OIL

The first of these shifts came toward the end of the Victorian period, when Edward Doheny first dug for oil in 1892 (an event described in detail earlier in this book). Within the next few decades, production peaked; by 1901, there were already 1,150 wells within the city's limits.

This unprecedented influx of wealth into Los Angeles rapidly shaped the city. A new aristocracy of sorts was created by the landowners and oil barons profiting from utilization of the city's natural resources. New

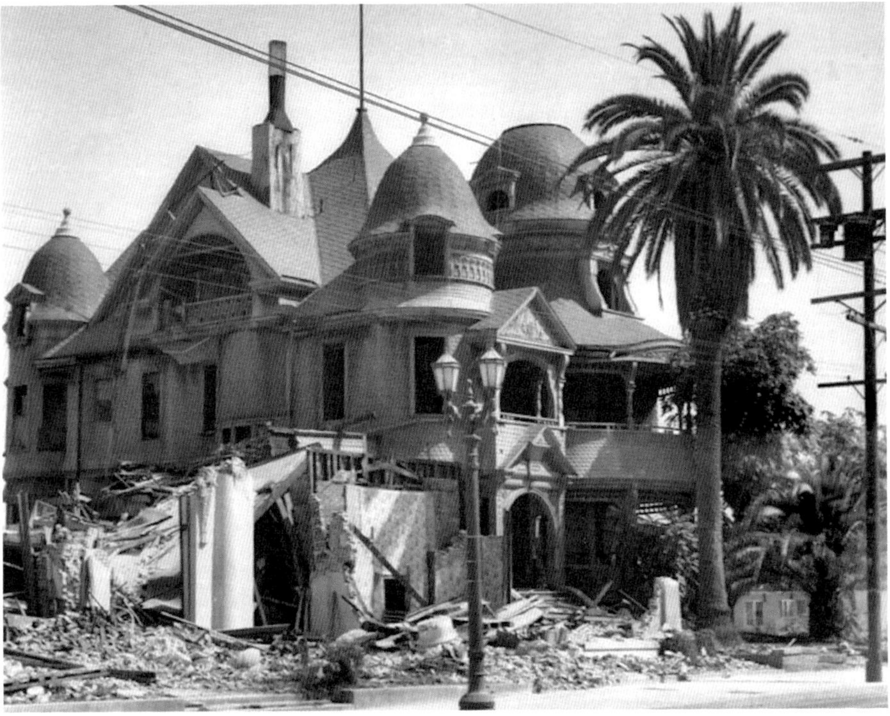

One of Bunker Hill's ornate mansions was later converted into the Melrose Hotel. Built in 1881, the Melrose is seen here just prior to its demolition in 1957. Countless buildings suffered similar fates during this era. *Courtesy the Los Angeles Public Library.*

mansions were constructed, new families rose in prominence and new businesses came into the city during the early years of the twentieth century. The Los Angeles of the previous century was rapidly fading away, replaced by an entirely new industry that was unheard of just several decades earlier.

The oil industry was also related to another major change in Los Angeles: the birth of car culture. The first automobile ever to drive in Los Angeles was in 1897; by the first few decades of the twentieth century, cars had become ubiquitous in the city. With cars and large-scale public transportation, getting around Los Angeles became much easier and stimulated the growth of new communities and suburbs.

MOTION PICTURES

In 1910, a young director named D.W. Griffith filmed a one-reel motion picture called *In Old California*. The movie ran only seventeen minutes and depicted life in California under Mexican rule. The film itself, including its plot and cast, was not particularly significant; the reason it is still remembered today is because Griffith filmed it in a small village called Hollywood.

Although originally sent to downtown Los Angeles by the Biograph Company to film several movies and determine whether California was a suitable home for a movie studio, Griffith found Hollywood to be much more scenic and hospitable for his filmmaking. Within several years of Griffith's trip, several major studios had relocated to the Los Angeles area, and in 1914, Cecil B. DeMille filmed the first feature-length film in Hollywood, *The Squaw Man*.

A large part of the movie industry's decision to relocate to Hollywood was the area's near-perfect weather; another less obvious factor was that film companies were trying to avoid taxes imposed by the Edison Film Company, which held many moviemaking patents. Regardless of the reasons for the move, its impact was immediate and widely felt. Aspiring actors and actresses, directors, studio executives and others in the industry flocked to the city, changing its demographics radically.

WATER

During the nineteenth century, Los Angeles used only water that was acquired locally, which proved to be a limiting factor on the city's growth. Downtown had yet to spread very far from the Los Angeles River, and suburbs were slow to develop due in large part to the lack of steady sources of water.

Beginning around the turn of the century, civic leaders began searching for new sources of water to promote the city's growth. The leaders of this movement, which culminated in the Los Angeles Aqueduct, were Frederick Eaton, mayor of Los Angeles from 1898 to 1900, and William Mulholland, superintendent of the Los Angeles City Water Company.

During the first years of the twentieth century, Eaton devised a plan in which snowmelt from the Sierras that collected in the Owens Valley would be diverted, by way of a gravity-powered aqueduct, to Los Angeles. Funding for the massive project began in 1905, and construction was started three years later. When it was finally completed in November 1913, it promised to change the city forever.

In addition to sparking the infamous Water Wars, forever immortalized in the 1974 film *Chinatown*, the aqueduct provided Los Angeles with enough water to allow for widespread civic growth. No longer confined by a semi-arid climate, the city was free to expand just as Eaton and Mulholland had hoped.

These three factors combined stimulated a massive population growth in Los Angeles. In 1880, the city had about 11,000 people; by 1900, that number had increased almost tenfold to more than 102,000. The population would more than triple in the next decade (319,000 in 1910) and again more than double before 1920 (576,000). In just forty years, Los Angeles had increased to fifty-two times its size in 1880.

Such changes in population inevitably brought other dramatic side effects to the city. New construction projects skyrocketed, and many buildings that had served the Victorian era perfectly were now outdated

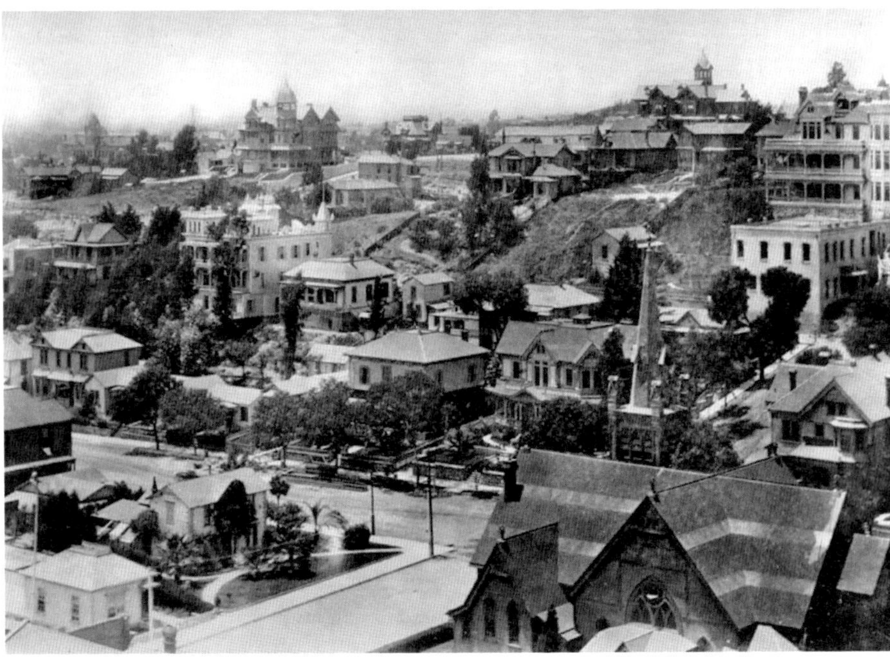

This 1890s view shows Bunker Hill dotted with Victorian homes, including the notable Crocker and Rose Mansions. During the twentieth century, nearly all of Bunker Hill's historic structures were demolished, and the hill itself was significantly leveled. *Courtesy the Los Angeles Public Library.*

and impractical. Traces of the nineteenth century were being wiped out at an unprecedented rate. The face of Los Angeles—downtown in particular—was radically being transformed.

Sheer population growth wasn't the only factor at play, however. Improved public transportation, including the founding of the Pacific Electric Railway and Los Angeles Railway in 1901 (coincidentally correlating with the end of the Victorian era), meant that the county was not only growing in numbers but in geographic size as well. In 1900, there were ten incorporated cities in Los Angeles; only thirty years later, that number had climbed to forty-two.

This urban sprawl would soon become synonymous with Los Angeles. The fact that so many communities were founded during the twentieth century is undoubtedly a major part of the reason why people do not associate the Victorian era with Los Angeles; in short, major parts of the county simply did not exist during that time. Many open spaces that were holdovers from the city's rancho days were victims of this growth, further obscuring the Los Angeles of the nineteenth century.

Perhaps the idea of "Victorian Los Angeles" is more of a picturesque image than a historical fact. Perhaps Los Angeles never fully developed into a Victorian city; maybe it only had elements of the Victorian era incorporated into itself without ever fully embracing the era.

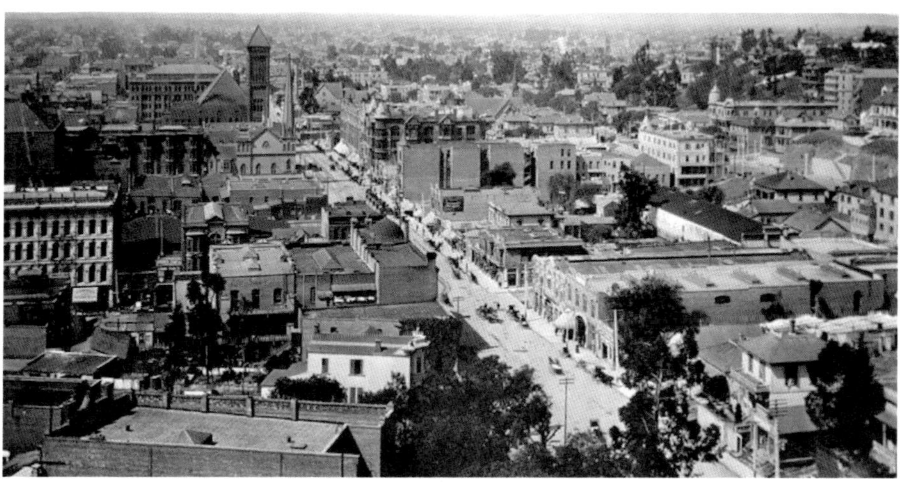

Taken from the County Courthouse, this photograph, looking south on Broadway in 1899, shows Los Angeles on the verge of the end of the Victorian era. Finally beginning to develop into a true metropolis, the city would undergo innumerable changes over the coming decades that would change the face of Los Angeles forever. *Courtesy the Los Angeles Public Library.*

On the other hand, it is remarkable that Los Angeles developed anything remotely resembling a Victorian culture. Here is a town that was, for all intents and purposes, part of the "Wild West." Los Angeles was all but isolated from the rest of the country before the arrival of the transcontinental railroad and remained remote for much of the twentieth century.

The fact that any influence—cultural, architectural or otherwise—from the East Coast (let alone Europe) was able to make a large-scale impact on such a place is truly remarkable. Los Angeles never could have developed into a truly Victorian metropolis on the order of New York or Chicago; instead, the city incorporated the Victorian era as simply another in a long line of influences dating back to the region's Spanish colonization.

The only thing that can be said for certain is that the Victorian Los Angeles is a thing of the past. So much of the city's identity—from its skyline to its industries to its culture—is deeply entrenched in the twentieth century, so much so that many residents have no sense of what the city was like during the Victorian era.

It is my hope that this book served as an effective introduction to Los Angeles during the nineteenth century, with a specific focus on that which is generally considered to be "Victorian" in nature. There is obviously much more to be written on the subject, as it is complicated and multifaceted; however, for the purposes of a brief foray into the era, I believe this book helps to document an extremely fascinating but woefully underrepresented time in the city's history.

Further Reading

Dawson, Jim. *Los Angeles's Bunker Hill: Pulp Fiction's Mean Streets and Film Noir's Ground Zero!* Charleston, SC: The History Press, 2012.

Epting, Charles. *University Park, Los Angeles: A Brief History.* Charleston, SC: The History Press, 2013.

Fogelson, Robert M. *The Fragmented Metropolis: Los Angeles, 1850–1930.* Oakland: University of California Press, 1993.

Roseman, Curtis C., et al. *The Historic Core of Los Angeles*. Charleston, SC: Arcadia Press, 2004.

Starr, Kevin. *Americans and the California Dream, 1850–1915.* Oxford, UK: Oxford University Press, 1986.

Wallach, Ruth, et al. *Historic Hotels of Los Angeles and Hollywood.* Charleston, SC: Arcadia Press, 2008.

About the Author

Born in Santa Monica and raised in Huntington Beach, California, Charles Epting is an undergraduate student at the University of Southern California studying history. He is the author of *A Brief History of University Park, Los Angeles* and *The New Deal in Orange County, California*, as well as the editor of *Orange County Pioneers: Oral Histories from the Works Progress Administration*. His research interest is in the Interwar Period, specifically President Franklin Roosevelt's New Deal, about which he has written numerous articles.

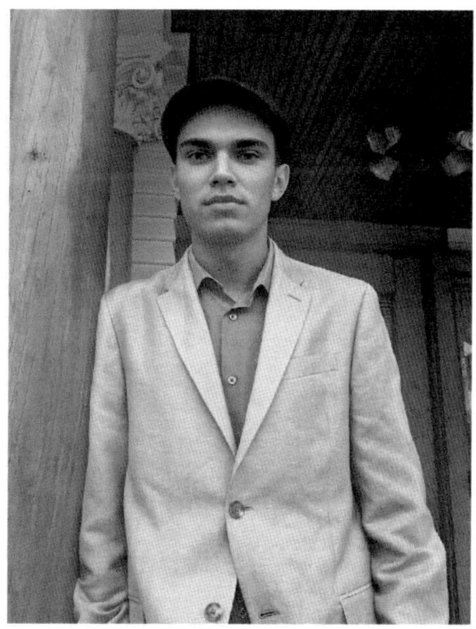